SEXUAL DIVISION OF LABOUR

The Engendered Labour Dynamics

SEXUAL DIVISION OF LABOUR

The Engendered Labour Dynamics

Dr. Suguna Pathy
Prof & Head
Department of Sociology
I/C. Director of Centre for the Study of
Social Exclusion and Inclusive policy
Co-ordinator of M.S.W Programme
VNSG University
SURAT

SERIALS PUBLICATIONS
NEW DELHI (INDIA)

First Published – 2011

ISBN: 978-81-8387-419-9

Published by

SERIALS PUBLICATIONS
4830/24, 1st Floor, Ansari Road
Darya Ganj, New Delhi-110002 (India)
Phone : 23245225. Fax : 91-11-23272135
E-mail: serials@satyam.net.in

Dedicated to

Tyna (Suma) & Papu (Sumit)

Contents

Acknowledgements

At the outset I wish to state that the present study has emerged out of a long struggle. However it finally took the present shape due to my determination as well as commitment.

At this juncture I pace on record my gratitude to the women for sparing their valuable time despite their tedious routine tasks and poor health. Being conscious and belonging to same gender I too share their concerns. Special thanks are due to Latha, Kantha, Saumya, Anitha, etc. for assisting me in this exercise.

I am also grateful to Prof. B.A.Prajapati, Vice-Chancellor, Veer Narmad South Gujarat University, Surat for support and encouragement in academic endeavours.

I sincerely acknowledge the critical insights I received from my late husband Prof. Jaganath Pathy who was also a well known scholar in Sociology/Anthropology on earlier draft. Meanwhile my children Tyna(Suma) and Papu(Sumit) despite their demanding professional and academic schedule stood by me as always been in extending not only moral support but also intellectual inputs. Indeed I have no words to express and thank stars for such wonderful children and above all kind humanbeings. The present work is dedicated to them.

Thanks are also due to the library Staff of Veer Narmad South Gujarat University and Centre for Social Studies, Surat, for lending cooperation during the study.

Last but not least I would like to thank Shri Vijay K. Patel, Smt. Purvi Vashi, Department of Sociology Veer Narmad South Gujarat University for typing the revised manuscript and formatting

Meanwhile all along I only tried to articulate the reflections with the objective reality in an effort to cognize the complex social processes. However the study suffers from shortcomings not only due to alienation from the masses but also time and professional as well as administrative constraints for which I owe sole responsibility.

Place : Surat
Date : January 28, 2010.

Suguna Pathy
Professor & Head
Department of Sociology,
Coordinator, MSW Programme
I/C Director, Centre for the study
of Exclusion and Inclusive Policy
VNSG University, Surat-395007

Prologue

Social graph reflects changes that have been taking place over a period of time revealing logic in events that can be compared and panoramically presented with regard to people, areas, institutions and epochs. Historically society and corresponding institutions are distinct creations of human adaptability. In course of chronological events that occurred in space and time, the emergence of cash economy followed by technological revolution altered the then existing collective notion to individualism. Consequently the shift in the organization of production gave rise to the development of productive forces, private property relations, family and state. The 'collective' was overtaken by 'individual', market economy and consumerism. Besides penetration of capitalism created sharp divisions between classes, communities, castes male and female clearly demarcating public and private. Social sciences, in particular anthropology and sociology adopted different perspectives to comprehend the historico-social dynamics of these domains and in the process more often than not gender relations were sidelined, as gender was not considered problematique. Barring a few exceptions the studies viewed family equivalent to procreation, sexuality and women in domestic ambit. Further the third world societies were projected as unchanging timeless entities that needed a tailored formula for change popularly known as 'modernisation package' without considering the structural context. In this connection nuclear family concept became the example of industrialization and kinship was considered diminishing. However many latter studies particularly in the context of migration indicated the prevalence of strong kinship network. It may be mentioned here that women's movement resulting in women's studies played a significant role in reconstructing the ethnocentric mind-set in social sciences. This does not however imply uniform approach in women's studies as there are diverse perspectives with regard to women's question.

Women constitute fifty percent of the total humankind and a major share of work force. Despite their total involvement in production their work is undervalued. More often women are perceived as householders not only by men but also by women due to specific patriarchal internalization processes. Meanwhile women belonging to tribal communities and lower castes were not strictly under the patriarchal ideology and cultural practices and even today they are less affected compared to the women belonging to the upper castes. In pre-capitalist economies household was the unit of production and so there was no strict division of labour between the sexes. However the scenario gets inverted with the penetration of capitalism generating sharp dichotomy between private and public spheres of economic activities. On the other side modern education enabled some women belonging to privileged strata to seek modern profession. At the same time the very modernization process marginalized a large chunk of both men and women, particularly women who were otherwise in traditional occupations like fishing, rice-processing, weaving, etc. Ultimately women bore the brunt of sexual segregation at work at lower wage level with the assignment of unskilled works. Viewing from this backdrop it is clear that the present direction of development is not people oriented to the enhancement of human caliber and to their reinforcement towards sustenance of humankind. It is essential to emphasize on quality of life which will give greater freedom, value and redemption from exploitative institutions. Precisely, as the notions of domesticity and sexuality i.e., patriarchal culture permeates the public realms and therefore to state policies too. Family being the centre of labour power women's question has to be analysed in terms of social relations of production.

Accordingly the following attempt in the ensuing pages is an effort to perceive the complexity of women's question from a wholistic point of view. At the very outset we admit that the study is plagued perhaps with 'inconsistencies' resulting in confusions and questions. However the researcher only hopes desperately that these very confusions might generate a critical critique tomorrow.

Introduction

Traditions across cultures and times over long periods often thought to be unchanged however do not remain frozen. Precisely nothing comes to us prestine through epochs. Historically the relationship if humankind to nature – the types of social organization, the level of productive forces, development of science, techniques and technologies have been the prime issues. Accordingly the social theories reflect these structural dynamics according to the prevalent social values corresponding to specific socio-economic formations. Thus in the recent past women have begun to question their position and value of their labour in the society. After reviewing the socio-political institutions specially in Third World societies one fact is certain that irrespective of change in regimes, sexual inequalities persist with little modifications, as women are continued to be oppressed and exploited with varying degrees. They constitute one-third of the total world's labour force, but they get only ten percent of the world's income. More often than not women are seen as objects of change than subjects of change and viewed as imitators than initiators. Despite constitutional privileges marked inequalities persist. In the wider politico-economic context in India disenchantment with the social order and the establishment is increasing; the legitimacy of protest and organized violence is being concealed and the repressive and persuasive role of the state is growing. Public investments, the expansion of the state of bureaucracy, police forces, new agricultural and industrial policies, privileges for the "weaker" sections, revamping the "old" system with a new policy of globalization, etc., has brought the vulnerable middle classes and also a section of the lower strata into the fold of the state. Nepotism, corruption, casteism, communalism, fundamentalism and sexism are the results of ever declining social morale. Accordingly we submit that violence against women has to be analysed within the broader quest of social justice, the unequal distribution of the means of production and the unequal relations between women and men. Any theoretical position which overlooks structural inequalities would be misleading and superficial. We argue that wherever injustice occurs it is a form of violence, it is this initial and primordial structural violence leads to the formation of a spiral of violence. Thus it is essential to re-examine vital and sensitive issues that directly concerned with the vast majority of the teeming millions of India who are living under subhuman, exploitative, oppressive and insecure circumstances. In this context caste and class in India become paramount to comprehend the future course of struggle towards liberation from the unjust social order and also patriarchal domination. The present exercise is an attempt in this direction.

The caste, class and gender nexus constitute the wider politico-economic structure and compels us to view in the context of historicity of Indian society. The dynamics of caste system, its survival, viability–and–flexibility- in the capitalist economy and polity is essentially a historical process. To beginwith the term caste is derived fro Portuguese which denotes race or lineage. Subsequently it was adopted in European languages to designate the rigid groups within society after the penetration of Portuguese in India, in the 16th century. Thus the term caste denotes both *Varna* and *Jati* (Dadhich 1986). However there is a specific distinction between the two. As Thapar observes that "the functional aspect of caste appears to have been *Jati* and not *Varna*. Varna appears to have represented a theory of structure, and may best be translated by the word "group". Jati relationships represent the actual way in which society functioned and this word is better translated as 'caste'. *Varna* became what sociologists have called "the ritual rank", whereas the jati was the indication of the actual status" (1975:29-30).

Be that as it may voluminous literature on Indian caste system exist denoting the Brahminical notion of purity and pollution, treating caste as a cultural category. A few empirical studies took refuge under modernization paradigm to analyse caste (Dube 1955; Beidelman 1959; Mayer 1960; Atal 1968; Srinivas 1969; Mandelbaum 1970; and Parvathamma 1971). However, several scholars have attempted to redress the balance which hither to had been heavily relied on culture. Meillassoux's work is worth mentioning here; he did not see class as a mere concomitant or adjust of industrialization and the formal <u>Varna</u> system is seen largely as an attempt or mechanism whereby class relationships are maintained in much the same way as they existed in the past (Meillassoux 1973). The present situation in India demands a substitution of sterile and abstract anthropological and sociological models towards an analysis of real subjects engaged in struggles. However, ultimately the peasants and the proletarians and historical actors, not merely transmission belts for an overdetermined set of conjunctures (Curie 1986). The British imperialism left far-reaching consequences on India social milieu by destroying the Asiatic society on one hand and establishing the capitalist relations on the other (Marx 1978: 32). The new land pattern created private property relations in British India by discarding hereditary rights. New transport system, communication system, politico-administrative and juridical structures and the new education system adversely affected the caste structure. Besides, it also was affected by rising nationalism, herald of industrialization to serve the colonial interests, emergence of national bourgeoisie and the formation of the working class. Thus colonial India witnessed the emergence of new classes which shook the specificity of the caste system. In continuation, the post colonial Indian society further became complex with increase in industrial capital, merchant capital, the growth of educated middle classes in bureaucracy, military and private sector, the rise of working class along with petty traders and unorganized labourers in the urban areas. While in rural areas the capitalist relations in agriculture gave rise to the rich peasants the nature of relations being dependent and comprised land lords, money-lenders, the tenants, the artisans and the landless agricultural labourers (Kamat 1979). The subsequent course of development in Indian society is marked by the expanded industrial production resulting in the formation of 'new class' of scientists, technocrates and bureaucrates on one side and the consolidation of power in the hands of rich peasants on the other. Thus the post colonial social conditioning influenced the caste system in various ways "but it would be far from the truth to suppose that caste has ceased to be a determinant of elite status in our country, even in our urban areas" (Sirsikar 1977: 74). On the contrary it is reinforced and perpetuated in new form for the survival of liberal democratic polity. With the increase in economic differentiation caste and class; higher castes members number more in exploiting classes and petty-bourgeoisie while low caste members comprise the vast toiling masses (Omvedt 1987). The agrarian relations are taking turn towards increasing of production resulting in the emergence of Kulaks while most of the artisans became middle peasants or agricultural labourers (conveniently). Caste is conveniently used as a weapon on untouchables or lower castes. Here the social relations between the ruling and subject classes become peripheral, if not vestigious. The untouchables become free agricultural labourers and organize themselves to which Kulaks through several dubious means (Pathy 1982). Crucial agrarian problems are conveniently reduced as cultural issues. It may be pointed here that uneven development of capitalism changes the form of caste, but does not erase it.

Perhaps a brief focus on caste and class in Indian history might throw some light on the course of peoples movements. It is held by some scholars that state created class in India while in most of the societies in the world class created state (Kosambi 1986). Hence the state-class nexus in Indian society poses some theoretical questions. Kosambi notes that class did not appropriate the surplus directly to sustain the state, on the contrary state directly appropriated to nurture the ruling class. Others feel that division of labour is a necessary condition for the production of commodities, but it does not follow conversely" (Brailly *et.al* 1981 : 32). The strongest base was caste which existed in Indian society, though "in theory there are four castes.... This theoretical system is roughly that of classes, whereas the observed castes and sub-castes are derived clearly from the tribal groups of different ethnic origins" (Kosambi 1970). Probably caste might have originated with the beginning of economic surplus in India and it was the means by which tribal societies were brought into the inequalities generated by the surplus. Thus caste came into existence much before the class formation, with the development of settled agriculture in the subcontinent, giving rise to Indus valley civilization (Klass 1980). In course of evolution, technological development and politics of accommodation there is a certain degree of economic differentiation within each caste group resulting in heterogeneity. Finally the new classes are amenable to the ruling classes and bring their caste members to their own advantage which directly helps to perpetuate the system. This marked differentiation impedes horizontal mobilization and transformation of "class-in-itself" to "class-for-itself". We hold that caste should be viewed primarily in its role in different social formations that have arisen in a chain of sequence. A social formation as it is based on the labour-process, arises after the producers in society are able to provide the surplus. Therefore it is doubtful to assume that caste existed before the division of labour. The *Purusa Sukta* in Rigveda is more is more a description of classes than castes; the *Brahmans* the priests; the *Vis* the people at large (chiefly peasants) and the *Sudras,* the service communities, does not show-either a heriditary division of labour or endogamy (Habib 1987). As we have mentioned elsewhere that caste came into being due to external pressures. Accordingly we infer the usage of the term *Jati,* as *Budha* is spoken of as belonging the *Sakya Jati* i.e. *tribe* (Wagle 1966 : 22-23). Being the rigid form of division of labour, the caste system formed part of the relations of production. The two basic features of early Indian village as Marx observes that (i) "the domestic union of agricultural and manufacturing pursuits within the village community ; and (ii) unalterable division of labour within the artisans and menials belonging to particular castes serving the entire village through customary rights (on payments) in kind or land allotments, dispensing with commodity exchange" (Marx 1938). The demiurgical labour sustained the self-sufficiency and the internal village economy, but certainly not the jajmani system as often thought to be and this enabled the ruling class to acquire the surplus. Consequently the village entered the commodity exchange economy. The hereditary occupation was transmitted from generation to generation (Marx 1938:331-2) and even prevented horizontal mobility. Caste system had two fold functions, (i) sustained the natural economy; and (ii) maintained class exploitation, not purity-pollution (Habib 1987). Accodingly we hold that caste and class co-existed since the inception of economic surplus and inequality. In pre-capitalist social structures the surplus was siphoned from the direct producers through organized caste system while the sub-caste formed the basic unit of kinship, jati the economic phenomenon (class) comprised the basic division of labour, thus caste nurtured and shaped the relations between the exploited and exploiting classes (Omvedt 1982). Caste and class could not be separated rather both were interwoven. In other words caste co-existed along with various modes of production to date the present, by changing its form. However we cannot identify caste merely with any single mode of production. Under capitalism caste and class get separated resulting in a complex admixture with regional variations reflecting the interdependent and interrelated influence on the power structure in India.

The movements and struggles both in the past and present encompass the questions of caste-class on one hand and gender on the other. The general assumption that the caste and class contradictions and gender inequalities get automatically resolved in the course of movements demands re-examination. The economic classes may disappear in socialism but the caste ideology, past classes, relations of production, and sexual inequalities will continue to persist till further course of transformation. Hence we may argue that the struggle against all these forms of oppression will continue even under socialism and it is conditioned by the concrete historical conditions and relations of production. Fighting caste and patriarchal values in the wider political economy and in daily life is a paramount aspect of the revolutionary movement and building peoples power (Omvedt 1987). This thesis raises two main issues i.e. whether cultural transformation and secondly whether caste is part of super structure or economic structure. Peoples history will ultimately decide this. As the productive forces develop over a period of time caste and class phenomena will accordingly increase with greater differentiation. In Indian context the social relationships based on caste with rigid hierarchy and occupational mobility, do not release the productive forces which influences the reduction of working class potential and underdevelopment of productive forces, thus reinforcing each other. Such a historical situation calls for a higher level of political intervention in socio-cultural areas besides politico-economic areas and this question has to emanate from the praxis based on experiences from the peoples movement. Meanwhile the intervention of state to preserve and strengthen the existing social relations in the interests of exploiting classes through various policies, anti-poverty programmes, affirmative policy, etc. is worth noting. These protective measures create new classes from among the scheduled castes to incorporate or assimilate into the ruling class fold. When once sufficient amount of horizontal distribution takes place by the process of co-option, the state would use the same protective measures to divide the people implicitly. Given the particular hierarchies of existing social order, it is all but inevitable that recruits from the subordinate classes into the upper crest, by the very fact of their entry into it, become part of the class which continues to dominate it (Pathy 1985). It is a glaring truth that the landreforms slowered the proletarianization while increasing class polarization. The anti-poverty programmes ended in agrarian crises and caste conflicts. Instead of sharpening the contradictions, this trend twists the course by giving birth to caste-class cleavages.

It may be observed that caste classes are perceived as mutually exclusive social phenomena. Caste and class can and do co-exist, and at the level of ideological legitimation caste reinforces economic relations of domination and subordination. Hence it is possible for the educated middle class women to enter into professions because the social groups to which they belong are from 'caste-oriented' to 'class-oriented' strategies for maintaining power and status (Liddle and Joshi 1986). Liddle and Joshi argue that gender divisions reinforce the caste divisions, but opine that class enables women to break caste by enabling the family to appropriate the social status of women's profession for the purpose of enhancing its own class position. Yet some others focus exclusively on professional women basing on sanskritization/ waternization model to link gender relations with caste-class phenomena (Caplan 1985). However we cannot solely rely on caste and class to explain the subordination of women as this varies from class to class (Omvedt 1975). For the vast masses of downtrodden class, caste, race, ethnicity and gender relations contribute to the process of sub-ordination. In this context, there is a positive hope emerging on the women's issue (Sharma 1985). It is argued that women from agricultural production are exploited at three levels (i) as women they are oppressed by their men belonging to same caste and class and through marriage transaction (ii) as women belonging to specific class by the land lords, rich peasants and moneylenders of exploiting class; and (iii) as women are sexually abused by the appropriated class. For the advancement of sociology of women in India, namely to analyse the degree of domination and subordination in different classes and castes it is but imperative to integrate the aforesaid three dimensions of women's exploitation both theoretically and empirically. These are vital issues not only to academia but also to the peoples struggles in a bid to challenge the system.

The reproduction and continuation of society rests on the reproduction of social life, within which nexus women constitute an important and potential actors in the entire process. Women's position in a society has to be viewed in relation to the basic social production and power and this varies from class to class. Accordingly we have to take into account the broader socio-economic and political implications of development, because as child bearers and rearer's women are directly concerned with prime human question which capitalism conveniently evades. Hence we emphasize that women's question is social question, not only women's. Historically, procreative process is shaped by the control of patriarchy and the ways in which gender categories are constructed varies according to mode of production in the society. Gender permeates socio-political and economic structures, thus gender categories are constructed varies according to the mode of production in the society. Gender permeates socio-political and economic structures, thus gender inequalities become integral constituents of social organization. Specific forms of oppression are articulated within the contextual structure of social relations of production. It may be noted that patriarchal household is the historical product of a prolonged and uneven process by which preexisting forces of subsistence relations get incorporated and adopted to the succeeding relations of production. Consequently forms of women's oppression are shaped by the politico-economic relations of domination and exploitation at large.

1

Sexual Division of Labour: An Appraisal

Sexual division of labour has been a significant social component since the evolution of human society. For, the work allocation by sex has been a near universal phenomenon throughout history with cross-cultural variations. Often the surveys on cross-cultural variations of sexual division of labour point out uniform nature of female work with regards to child-care (Murdock 1937; Murdock and Provost 1973; Brown 1970). Notwithstanding these uniformities the ethnographic record a degree of variation (Esticko-Griffin and Griffin,1981) where it is observed that Agta women (foragers) join men in fishing and hunting. In exceptional cases women were also found to be warriors. This and other rarities according to some (Rosaldo, 1974) is due to women's less pre-occupation in child-care and lactation than otherwise. Thus the chores are separated as *domestic* (private) and *outside* (public) along sex lines.

In this context ethnographic record reveals welter of diversity. Precisely as gender identities and gender-related behaviour patterns are not constituted uniformly in all societies as cross-cultural comparisons point out substantial variations. However the structural mechanism primarily responsible for male/female habits is the sexual division of labour as Bourdeiu (1977:33) observes that ".....the awakening of consciousness of sexual identity and the incorporation of the dispositions associated with a determinate social definition of the social functions incumbent on men and women come hand in hand with the adoption of a socially defined vision of the sexual division of labour". For in a male dominated society men occupy mega space while women are pushed to periphery corresponding to their spatially separate spheres of activity. Sexual division of labour vary in their undimensionality, their rigidity and their clarity even while maintaining a general pattern across a wide variety of cultures"(Parker and Patterson 1993.32). This variation is produced by the rigidity of sexual division of labour whether the work is "prescribed" or "preferred".

In pre-capitalist societies subordination of women is kinship-ordered as there is predisposition to male control which is embedded in the pre-capitalist relations at home, in the field and in the production sphere (with the landlord peasant or capitalist; Wood 1988). The biggest question before women's movement all over is how to unite as they are vertically divided. Subsequently this raises the issue of relationship between the feminist movement and other social movement. The fact is women are united by sexist oppression and simultaneously divided by class society.

Be that as it may, sex is a biological context while gender is cultural- a set of learned behaviour patterns. In common usage sex refers to sexual instincts, desires of related manifestations. This hydraulic model of sexuality holds that these desires often undermine a drive or an instinct leading to search of sexual gratification (Caplan,1987:1). Mention may be made that sexual behaviours and practices, morality and ideology are constantly in state of flux. The point is to differentiate sexuality from gender and a need to explore the articulation between the two (Vance, 1984b). Accordingly seclusion of women takes place in various forms in different cultures. Seclusion or 'Purdah' has visible and invisible restrictions and regulates women's activities within and out of household. In brief seclusion controls women's sexuality and ritual status specially in pre-capitalist social formations. However we cannot attribute this entirely to caste structure without noting cross-cultural variations and their significance. For some stereotypes are intellectually pejorated.

As we know ideologies are historically defined phenomena controlling human thought and behavior. Seen this way ideology of housewification underlines as one of the structural features of patriarchy and enhances the unequal division of labour in the household. The housewife ideology or patriarchal ideology categorises all women's work as an extension of her role as dependent and unpaid householder which is a cultural interpretation of work (Mies, 1980). More often women's work is underpaid and undervalued. Accordingly household production perpetuates seclusion controlling women's sexuality and at times is internalized as status symbol. Secondly seclusion enhances women's isolation and the home-based production becomes disorganised. It may be mentioned that in pre-capitalist relations of production exploitation is carried through oppressive relations of reproduction. Not surprisingly capitalist development widens the gender gap in its own interest as specific exploitative relations of caste, class and gender jointly perpetuate the seclusion and control female sexuality.

The rapid rise of women's movement both at home and abroad has generated a mass of literature about women on different aspects both theoretical and empirical. However in India by and large the swing is towards the latter. The academic area known as Women's Studies has been established during the eighties to evolve more knowledge of hitherto invisible women, their work and their role in society in course of social history. These studies are drawing a considerable attention of social scientists, planners, activists and various political parties to the unequal position of women in society and the subsequent problems despite legal and constitutional privileges. At this juncture we submit that gender discrimination not only prevails in socio-ideological realms but also in academic domain reflecting *a priori* assumption and stereotypes.

Increased dialogue between the women activists and academia raised an umpteen number of crucial issues pertaining to theory and conceptual framework in women's studies. Broadly there are three major schools of thought namely, radical feminism, socialist feminism and marxist/

materialist feminism which have questioned the existing theoretical constructs and assumptions in social research. Accordingly radical feminism universalises women's oppression as the male drive for power in consequence of women's biological role of reproduction. This way it reduces women's position in society to sexual and cultural determinism-leading to teleological, ahistorical and mechanistic interpretations. While socialist feminism holds that sexual hierarchy is rooted in ideological interpretations which men relegate to sexual differences and is finally gets institutionalised in the family. This approach however fails to accord material basis for women's oppression and argues that patriarchy is maintained because it is a functional requisite in capitalism. This view also observes that patriarchy is autonomous in capitalism. In other words it is based on a spurious teleology assuming that social system exists and functions to maintain equilibrium and status-quo. This approach not only fails to explain the internal logic of patriarchy but also negates historical dynamics while upholding functionalistic dimension of patriarchy. Marxist feminism traces women's oppression and subordination in the family and labour process i.e. the social relations of production and reproduction. This approach holds that patriarchy is a general hierarchical structure of sexual relations; precisely because males control women's labour power and women's reproductive capacity. Every society divides and specializes labour tasks to some degree for efficiency and survival. In history with the development of productive forces and ensuring complex division of labour, the surplus was appropriated by men as their private property. Subsequently this resulted in the institution of monogamous marriage and family to legalise inheritance. Thus the wife came under the control of the husband. In due course patriarchy gradually became a historically specific institution of labour in household unit of production. In class societies the entire labour process, the thinking and creative experience of the whole person (men as well as women) is nullified. The production and reproduction of labour power takes place substantially within the family through the labour of the housewife and hence her labour is an important generator of surplus value. The relations of domestic labour differ in different classes, under different modes of production. Here comes the sexual division of labour and its articulation with patriarchy and the prominent mode of production be it capitalism, pre-capitalism or its combination. It is also important to take this cognition at politico-ideological levels in the wider context.

In the present study an attempt is made to bring the linkage between the household and economy in order to understand women's work. In this context we have analysed the domestic relations(family relations) and work to understand the variation of women's oppression. In course of our study we found that male dominance is not subjective relations or prerogative of men *per se* and is rooted in the social relations of production and the relative position of men and women within these relations. From this we have derived that specific forms of oppression of women prevail in different classes. In the present enterprise we made a humble effort to conceptualise sexual division of labour within the framework of capitalist mode. This is precisely due to the fact that certain forms of women's oppression are structurally embedded within specific social relations and hence they become inseparable from the process of social reproduction and are historically contingent and structurally conditioned. It needs no mention that family is not an aberration; it is a historical necessity of the organization of society to ensure domination in which exist private property and the division of people into classes. Thus family in a class society is an economic unit and perpetuates the existence of class divisions (Jennes 1972). While women's oppression begins in the family it however provides or appears to have a private concern than social. It may be argued that we cannot generalize family in class society. For women generate two types-one the future means of production and the other future labourers. In other words subordination of women needs to be analysed in the specific context of historical conjecture. This necessarily calls for the analysis of social relations of production.

In the following a brief sketch of the review of concerned literature is presented to have a broader understanding of the problem. The objective of the literature survey is to arrive at theoretical stand. A large mass of literature on various dimensions concerning women exists in India with diverse approaches while most of the studies by and large fall under descriptive category. Undoubtedly women's studies is increasing albeit descriptively despite the withdrawal of official grants as well as publicity and this could be possible only due to women's movement at various levels. The civil rights movements, ecological movements and various massive mobilizations on various women's concerns have helped to create a political climate conducive to women beginning to question their role in society culminating into women's movement. In this context we argue that women's studies is not a mere matter of women with personal problems, but examine the social phenomena which have gone virtually unchallenged, if not unnoticed until the development of women's movement. As knowledge is power and so to collect knowledge about ourselves is an indispensable weapon in our struggle for liberation.

Gender hierarchy predates capitalism. The latter intensifies exploitation based on caste, class and gender while freeing mainly male labour and maintain the reproduction of labour force without any price to capital (Deere,1979).Capitalism brings women into wage work but the unequal division of domestic labour does not transform in the process. Meanwhile it may be mentioned that the debate on production and reproduction is yet to be resolved. However, for now we take a position taken by Harris and Kate (1981). Accordingly we define social reproduction as a specific historic process by which the specific set of social relations in a particular social formation are reproduced and perpetuated. While *human reproduction* comprises the institutional range of marriage, kinship, fertility and sexuality and the process of child bearing under male dominance controlling sexuality culminating to gender subordination (Beneria,1979). As regard to *reproduction of labour* it is process of replacing and socialising the children to be future working class. Therefore, it is paramount to analyse the "system of allocation of agents to positions within the labour process on the basis of sex , and lastly a system of reinforcement of social construction of gender" in order to comprehend the gender subordination (Young, 1978:125). Thus for operational we define patriarchy as a particular set of social relations that enable men to control women's labour power as well as fruits of her labour (production and reproduction). It is a specific historical form of household relationship and societal ideology. Therefore patriarchy is not autonomous, on the contrary there exists a dialectical relationship between sex and class.Masculinity and femininity refer to class and sex between specific nature of familial and class ideologies and these are reproduced and operated in various institutions and practices each with internal contradictions. Patriarchy oppresses women by controlling their fertility and sexuality. The oppression of women has not just come out due to capitalism. For the sexual division of labour and the male control of women predates capitalism (Rowbotham 1973). Power relations between men and women are obscured within the problematique of sexual division of labour.

Meanwhile state intervention through economic reforms and policies in agriculture and industry further intensifies the already existing uneven development of capitalism thereby debarring access to resources which eventually forces both men and women to sell their labour power so as to ensure their own social reproduction. Furthermore state intervention also creates domestication of women as housewife and home-makers by introducing handicrafts and home-based production. Unequal relations of production reflect in unequal gender relations. Then it follows that ever increasing responsibility of the rural women (due to male migration in cities) signifies the maintenance of unequal sexual division of labour. The rural women's labour has been refrained according to specific class and gender structures at different historical periods (Brycasas and Mbilin 1979). For domestic labour is socially useful and therefore is crucial, operating in the specific area of personal relations.

More often than not sexist patterns go unnoticed as they are deeply embedded in our minds so much so that we are hardly aware unless they become a problem. They become part of our social world in pervasive ways. It is only recently sociologists and anthropologists have begun to study gender as sociological issue. Personal/private have their origins in the public issues that emerge from specific historical and social conditions. People live in interaction with their social and physical environments; in this process human consciousness is formed by the interplay between people as subjects and objects in the world of their living. Viewed thus the movement of human history involves continuous creation and recreation of human life. According to Engels (1972) production and reproduction form the central features of human society. Marx and Engels observe that the first division of labour was by sex for the purpose of propagating children i.e., gender thus becomes the first class antagonism; however this this thesis is left only at this stage.

Sexism as an ideology justifies the power of men over women. The extent to which women believe in the precepts of sexist ideology is nothing but reflection of the power of coercion and social controls besides internalisation process. Therefore it is argued that sex difference in childhood socialization serves to reproduce existing sexual divisions in society (Griffiths and Saraga 1979). However, liberal struggles for certain rights though not for complete emancipation as Lenin pointed out "is always struggle for reforms as part of its activities, though it subordinates the struggle for reforms as a part to the whole, to the revolutionary struggle for freedom and socialism" (Lenin 1969:62). It may be mentioned that subordination of women in sexual relations was not a necessary consequence of the biological fact that women bear children; rather it is to confirm undisputed paternity to own the increasing surplus wealth (Engles *Op. Cit.*: 125). We reiterate that biological reproduction of women in conjunction with the development of private property shapes the existing divisions between the sexes of the working class and also middle class though in varying degrees (Humphries 1981). Besides female participation in the labour market due to the penetration of foreign capital into the third world countries, also created new forms of subordination.

At this juncture we submit that the relations of household with the economic systems, the concurrent changes and as to how they are determined and reinforced need to be investigated and we will be undertaking this exercise in the forthcoming cross-cultural study of India, Iran and Syria. Precisely the changes in different modes of production influence the pattern of kinship structures which ultimately define and determine the position of women in the whole process of production and reproduction. The dynamics of household organization in conjunction with the formal (paid) and informal(unpaid) economies and social relations in production ultimately determine the kinship pattern. The emergence of market economy and the accompanied changes in the organization of production has direct bearings on the organization of households and family structures. Very often in precapitalist societies kinship systems serve as both economic and cultural determinants and the link between agrarian and industrial network is continued under such conditions. The advent of market exchange ultimately determine the structure and function of household in terms of politico-economic and intra and inter households within the community. In self-subsistence economies with the alternation to exchange economy, the production system was created and modified through individual and kin divisions. The implication of this transformation within the private sphere of household can be understood only by analyzing the kinship relations and the kind of exchanges (Marx 1897). Mention may be made that exchange of goods and services among the kinfolk is an integral part of pre-capitalism. Exchange of work and goods in some tribal communities are not paid but are *reciprocal*. While in the exchange economy the exchange value of the product or service and the cost of goods and services emphasises the changes in kinship structures. Because the produce ceases to regard his/her product in terms of its use value and instead goes for exchange value, i.e., it is no longer for personal needs and its exchange value goes up with the increased division of labour and the creation of cash economy in social relations (Marx 1887 : 146).

Be that as it may household is a three dimensional unit in the social organization of production.

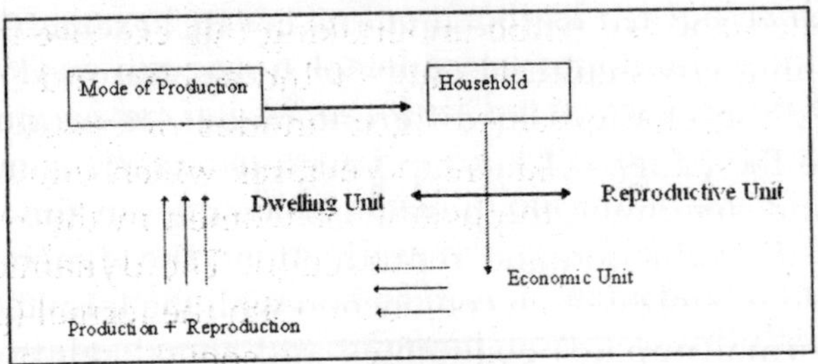

Figure 1

Household as domestic groups share production and reproduction both social and biological. For family is not an organic whole but a hierarchical system and so parenthood and kinship are not natural but are essentially social institutions. Women perform housework and undertake child, sick and aged care not because they are natural, but for security. Men and women have equal rights as legal and political citizens. As persons they have equality before law, but freedom of choice of partner is restricted, despite of constitutional provisions. While family opposes this freedom, state does not intervene. Besides family does not also ensure the security for women, divorced and widows, rather suppresses them. Thus individuals in families, households, lineages, gender, castes, classes and communities coexist and we cannot keep them in separate compartments. Arguments and counter arguments only legitimise the family hierarchy but do not explain. Who does what in the family is regulated by tradition and by the class position. The distribution of work within the family depends on labour market. Thus social reproduction becomes household activity involving entire network of kin relations (Goody, 1972). The housework in a household is an ensemble of activities involving cooking, washing, cleaning, fetching water, fodder, fuel and the like besides childcare and nursing the sick and the aged. For the operational part we define housework as the dynamics of labour spent in production and reproduction in daily consumption. Some studies analyse housework as a commodity generator and augmenting surplus value in capitalism (Dalla Costa and James 1972; Rapp 1978; Vogel 1979; Zaretsky 1976). The political and economic positioning of households in the wider network demand urgent analysis, precisely as kinship structures possess political potential in controlling production. Social relations of production criss-cross and tie the kinship structures in terms of their relation to production (Sanjek, 1982: 99). This would enable us to comprehend the position of women and their oppression. Under capitalism kinship relations are replaced by juridicopolitical structure of the state where the former becomes subordinate, existing as only cultural apparatus and losses control over production process. Productive labour is separated from kin relations. In pre-capitalist societies kinship denotes a set of practices constituting immediate reproduction of social order. Power is held by male heads of households and there is a clear separation of private and public in pre-capitalist societies. In addition, in the private spheres of household, the patriarch enjoys power over all junior males, women and children; while in the public sphere he shares power along with other patriarchs according to his economic relations in the social structure. Females are prevented from entering this public life; with in the household they may influence the males informally. Therefore it is necessary to investigate the bases of women's power and their relationship with the organization of production.

Meanwhile the issue regarding the bases of women's subordination to men does not merely revolve around the question of formal economic and political power, but it is the subtle social control excercised over men and women specially the latter (Campbell 1980; Meillassoux 1981; Saddawi 1980; Morokvasasic 1981). Thus women are trapped in inescapable practices and cannot even have spatial mobility. Furthermore, in many societies a women's social position depends on bearing children, specially males. There is a polemical relationship between the population growth and economic growth i.e the women's sexuality.

In most of the third world countries age and sex constitute prime categories of the division of labour (seniority). This enforces the interdependence of family labour and this type of division of labour is legitimised and is continually perpetuated by a specific set of norms which in turn ensure gender identity. The gender based works incorporate cultural assessment of their social value, legitimising the unequal distribution of the products of labour in the household(Roberts 1981). The question of women's right of self-determination of her sexuality is fully ignored. More often social explanations are given natural foundations and as a result social sciences directly or indirectly assume that the world consists wholly or sufficiently of men and that women are extras, the detached reproduction organs of men or a lumpen group (Beechy and Allan, 1982). Studies reveal that lines of class divisions and conflicts run between and that the position of the family as a whole within the system of stratification..." derives from that of the family "head"... the separation of sex roles within the family being itself the expression of a major forum of inequality existing between the sexes " (Goldthrope 1983 : 468-469). Thus the oppression and subordination of women is an integral part of the exploitation and production of the society in general. Interestingly in a very usual cultural representation of gender diversities in the society, only one gender represents as both part and whole, while the other minority and specific. Thus everyday language usage amply reveals the content clearly; for an instance, 'man' and 'humanity' become synonymous, while women never become general, never universal, but are only particular, only located in relation to men.

In the final analysis people make history, albeit within objectively determined conditions, for social laws do not operate like natural laws. It seems unequal development is universal, history ultimately is history of class struggles between male and female. Because class relations define dialectically the modes of production, constituting successive social formations, corresponding to different levels in the development of productive forces. Social reproduction cannot be understood only internally, but also in its relations with imperialism and at the level of state in economic regulation. Therefore, we argue that to consider patriarchy as relatively autonomous is ahistorical. Because when mode of production changes the patriarchy also undergoes change accordingly. Secondly, the simplistic reduction of patriarchy to sexuality, marriage and domestic life is to deny the inherent contradictions and change. Precisely patriarchy as a set of social relations has a material base by which men control women's labour power. This control is perpetuated by excluding women from the access to economic resources and also by restricting women's sexuality. For, more often than not power is held by males and there is a distinct separation of private and public

Methodology

The relationship between objective and subjective well being, in short, is far from isomorphic. Changes in sex-role stereotypes, women's labour participation, female headed households and male migration reflect on women and work (Crosby, 1982). As researcher's conclusions depend on the research objective and strategies have only tried to be explicit about the assumption that we began, the method we used in collecting the data. However, all this is shaped and influenced whether directly or indirectly by the world outlook at large, the ideological orientation. Our aim is to reach the professional and the general and in all fairness we must admit that we cannot think of reaching the people due to our alienation, who are the basis of this research. We only would feel satisfied if we are able to focus the people and their issues in the ensuring pages.

There is seemingly close relation between the theory and methods of investigation. The social differentiation makes total participation makes difficult for the investigation; but one can overcome little with social sensitivity (Goody, 1976). For instance single migration take place due to rural poverty, better wages, employment opportunities, to procure enough dowry and so on. Besides pressing economic needs , the workers are under pressure to help the sibling's marriage or even their own marriage, constructing house and paying off the debts. After the marriage or the consumer demands of the worker's parents or affines are met, he/she is back in town for urban employment. In this ongoing process he/she shuttles to and fro (village-town-village) to meet the growing needs of his/her family. In the meantime the worker tries to accumulate rural capital in the form of livestock, additional piece of land or any such equipment. Thus by late forties the workers are back to their native place in the village, to give rise yet another migrating cycle by their children, mostly male children, first by the eldest son followed by the others. In the whole process class awareness is subordinate to ethnic consciousness in the urban centre where the workers have migrated. Rigid division of labour underpins the institution of marriage and in turn marriage reinforces the allocation of work by sex; it is one way of structuring asymmetrical exchange of labour. The discrepancy between cultural norm and social practice is by no means only a product of colonial culture contact and an expression of the frequently described ambivalence of intellectual suffering from neo-colonialism (Mies, 1980).

It is a fact that since the early time, people have been migrating in search of work and also better paid work from backward regions to developed or economically viable regions not only to ensure survival rate but also to raise standard of living and quality of life. As we know this mobility takes place at two levels (i) The movement of labour and (ii) The movement of capital. More often regional disparities determine the degree of migration and the corresponding process. In this context migration process can be comprehended with reference to the level of development of capitalism. Secondly the phenomenon of migration is generated by inherent structural factors. Particularly in third world countries unequal industrialization enhances movement of capital and sustains it. Under these conditions unorganised sector co-exists with organized sector while absorbing a large chunk of unskilled and semi-skilled work force. The proletarianisation process varies from society to society which involves the separation of agricultural producers from ownership and control of land also from usurfructury rights. However this alone does not necessarily reflect the industrialisation process in most of the third world countries like in the Pacific, Asia and Africa where men migrate to towns seeking temporary or long term employment while leasing their families behind in the villages to safeguard their land rights. The apparent reasons are the low wages and the cost of living far below the levels on which families can survive, the accommodation problem and insecurity perhaps results in this situation. In this way the capitalist mode of production bolsters its own profit by necessitating them to meet the cost of social reproduction. Consequently job insecurity forces the worker to maintain their land as an ultimate security (Cheater, 1989).

Meanwhile the strength of data collection lies in using diverse methods in social research. Accordingly we have used various qualitative techniques according to the demand of situation in the field, besides interview schedule, participant observation, case study method and so on. Precisely as "methods are not an end in itself but means to gain better understanding of the insight into the problem under investigation, and secondly that the techniques of gathering data and analysis are relative tio the nature of the problem of research" (Rao, 1986 :171). For any scientific inquiry it is essential to go beyond surface view to the essence of things. Because mere description of the phenomenon is not sufficient to show that they are well-established regularities itself (Russell and Ury, 1982). However, observations alone cannot yield data, particularly with regard to different behaviour patterns unless the investigator is 'committed'.

Hypotheses

In the present exercise we have attempted to analyse domestic relations and the production process to understand women's oppression. Our objective is to probe the structural account of social relations of production and the relative position of men and women within these relations. For, the production the reproduction of labour power takes place substantially within the family through the labour of the women and hence her labour is an important generator of surplus value. This does not mean that relations of domestic labour are uniform in pre-capitalism and capitalism. Here lies our effort to understand sexual division of labour and its articulation with patriarchy and the related mode of production. Patriarchy refers to a specific historical form of household relationship and socio-cultural ideology. This way patriarchy draws the attention to some of the forms in which sexual division of labour is reproduced by what is called "subterranean status" between men and women. Precisely in the ultimate analysis the structure of political economy at the wider level reinforces the associated relations be it in the family or at the work place. Certain forms of women's oppression are structurally embedded within specific social relations, and hence they become inseparable from the process of social reproduction and hence are historically contingent and structurally conditioned. Accordingly the following hypotheses were evolved for the study:

- dominant social relations of production determines specific patriarchal relations and the oppression of women varies accordingly;
- under pre-capitalism domestic labour (paid and unpaid) encounters structural constraints and the dynamic potential of women is repressed;
- while in capitalism , higher the productive force level complex is the sexual division of labour i.e., women's labour power is appropriated both in family and in production process.

The study was undertaken in Limbayat and Dumbal slum regions in Surat City predominantly inhabited by migrant labour from different states in textile industry. We have selected Limbayat and Dumbal for our study because of the heavier concentration of the migrant textile workers from Andhra Pradesh. Secondly, the rationale of this selection as the universe of study is that the researcher is from Andhra

Pradesh on one side and on the other living in Surat since three decades and hence enjoys the relative advantage of cognition of the city's economy, polity, culture and the labour movement to Surat from Andhra Pradesh, Orissa, Uttar Pradesh, Maharashtra and Bihar respectively. Furthermore the researcher was also associated in a survey report on "Working and Living conditions of the Surat Textile Workers" directed by Gujarat High Court in 1984 and thus is familiar with the people in the area. We have tried to analyse the degree of women's oppression, the process of their economic participation, the formation process of identity, internalization and domesticity and the like. At the micro-level we have analysed these associated processes with the help of general household census and individual schedules, participant and non-participant observation methods, case study, both individual and group interview methods, as the situation demanded. To trace the other spectrum of women's question and inequality in wider context, we made a brief attempt to analyse the political economy of Andhra Pradesh through secondary source material.

A sample of 500 Telugu female workers engaged in jari textiles and domestic labour both paid and unpaid were interviewed randomly for our investigation purpose. It may be mentioned here that the women migrant workers to Surat have come only through male migration and not the vice-a-versa. The female migration to Surat is co-ordinated by the social arrangements of marriage. In the present study we tried to understand how different modes viz., pre-capitalism and capitalism articulate and co-exist along side. Secondly we have only attempted to trace the sexual division of labour within the given context of mode of production. In this connection we wish to mention that the study is laced with confusions and shortcomings partly due to the degree of the problem and partly due to alienation from the objective reality. However we have only tried to cognize the complex realities in our quest.

Surat in due course of history embraced accompanying changes in economy, polity and culture rendering a composite configuration to the city. The demographic profile of Surat is accordingly undergoing considerable changes particularly since the recent decades interms of absolute as well as relative progression. As regard to the spatial distribution the highest growth is recorded in Ahmedabad district (74.8% urban) and Surat (50.6%) (Das 1994; Pattanayak 2001; Report of the Department of Sociology) The absolute increase of urban growth rate in Surat is as high as eight per cent by 90s and 11% by 2005 respectively. Among all the districts in Gujarat the growth rate of urban population is Surat is 62.29% during 1991-2001 the highest next only to Gandhinagar. It is a fact that majority of the people live in Surat City alone clearly denotes the availability of economic opportunities. This is a corollary to the growth distribution and concentration pattern of industrial workers in Surat. Available data reveal that Surat ranks third in Gujarat interms of average number of daily workers in the factories. Surat has a large number of unregistered small and home based industries articulating with the organized industrial sector. These unregistered units invariably employ a large chunk of migrant labour. Mention may be made that Surat is second in line in hosting non-agricultural establishments in the State. Besides large manufacturing units like ferilisers, man made synthetic fiber, paper pulp, cement, yarn, textiles, inorganix chemicals, petrochemicals, petroleum products, iron and steel, industrial machinery, etc. are located in and around Surat.

Surat absorbs a wide range of industrial labour and other allied service sector, also exhibits petty trade and business activities like hawking, vending, carting. etc. In this connection it may be mentioned that Surat reached the zenith of fame through trade and commerce during the middle of sixteenth century. Surat City's economy continues with jari and art silk industries besides diamond cutting and it's associated production processes, falling under the unorganized sector. This is possible by subdividing the units to avoid the Factory Act, 1947.Presently the city is the centre of manufacturing trade and commerce with a variety of industrial units located at Udhna Udyognagar, Baroda Rayan and GIDC, along side capital intensive manufacturing and processing pockets in

Hazira consisting large companies like Reliance, Larsen & Turbo, Essar Steel, Kribco, Oil and Natural Gas Commission and the Indian Oil Corporation respectively. This way the steady pace of industrialization and the industrial development policy of the state government recorded a fast number of industries and attracted a large chunk of migrant workers from different states.

In order to perceive the problem from a larger angle we will be examining the socio-political history of Andhra Pradesh in the following chapter.

2

Andhra Pradesh : A Note

Andhra Pradesh is known as the state of rivers. Over thirty-five rivers flow across the state ; two of them are the biggest in the South – The Godavari and The Krishna. The other three important rivers are the Vamsadhara, the Nagavati and the Pennar, all of them flow into bay of Bengal forming fertile deltas. The land between Godavari and Krishna is one of the most prosperous regions in the country, known as the granary of South Coastal Andhra, is named after these river East Godavari district, West Godavari district and Krishna district respectively. Andhra Pradesh is the fifth largest state in India, with the total area of 2,76,754 sq.kms. The state was initially carved out of the composite state of Madras and later nine Telangana districts (former Hyderabad State) were added to it in 1956. Geographically the state extends over parts of the deccan plateau and the eastern coastlands. The state can be divided into three distinct economic and geographical regions; the fertile and prosperous coastal Andhra (the Circar region), the stony dry and backward Rayalaseema (also known as 'Rallaseema', region of stones in Telugu) and the rocky, dry and backward Telangana region respectively. The latter two regions contain red soil which cannot retain moisture for cultivation. However parts of Telangana districts contain fertile black soil. Main crops are paddy, millets, oil seeds, chilies, fruits specially mangos, pulses, castor, sugarcane, etc. Tabacco and cotton are important commercial crops grown in the state, the best Virginia tobacco in India comes from Guntur district.

The state has share in producing pulses at the national level at 8.6% while in food grains it is 8.7%, in oil seeds 12.9% and in sugarcane 5.5% respectively. Each family has a name of its own, which is generally either the name of the village where one's ancestors lived or the name of the vocation one follow. It is prefixed to one's firstname and is called as Inti Peru (House name) in Telugu. The communities like Reddis, Kamamas and Kapus belonging to Sudra caste dominate the core of socio-economic and political spheres in the state, a factor which is significant to comprehend the social dynamics and its associated ramifications.

Historically, it is said that the Andhras represent the earliest Aryan migration to the Peninsula. The name *Andhra* was first mentioned over 3,000 years ago in the Aitreya Brahmana. From the third century B.C. the Andhra empire extended over a large portion of India as far as Pataliputra. The Andhra Kingdom reached its zenith under the Satavahanas, when Andhras traveled along the two rivers to migrate to the east coast, establishing in the process such renowned centres of learning as Amaravati (in the present Guntur district) and Nagarjunakonda. This is the most significant epoch in the history of Andhra. The first capital of Satavahanas was Srikakulam. Mahayana Buddhism flourished during their reign and Acharya presided over the world university at Sriparvata *(Rao 1975)*. Then came the Chalukyan Kings followed by Kakatiyas in twelfth century with Warangal as their capital extending their frontier upto Nellore, for nearly two centuries. The political power of Andhra Pradesh was mainly in the Deccan and not outside, through the centuries. After the fall of Kakatiyas in 1310 A.D. to the Sultanate of Delhi, two mighty empires viz., the Brahamani and the Vijayanagar empires sprang up in Deccan. With the fall of Brahmani empire at Gulbarga, the Qutubshahis of Golconda consolidated Telugu speaking area from Srikakulam in the north to Golconda in the South-west; thus the dynasities in Andhra is interwined with the Qutubshahi dynasty in 15th century; followed by another Moghul ruler Asafjahi under Farukh Siyar, the Moghul King in Delhi. The latter appointed Chin Kilik Khan one of his best generals as Subedar of Deccan. After Siyar's death in 1719 the Subedar assumed the title of Nizam-ul-Mulk established in Deccan, down to Hyderabad which is the herald of Nizam rule in Andhra Pradesh.

The Viyayanagar empire under Krishnadevaraya (1509-1530) extended almost the entire region upto the boarders of Orissa. With the appearance of East-India Company in India, which established its fort at Machilipatnam on the east coast, the Nizam of Hyderabad surrendered circas forcibility. In the battles between the French and the English, the East India Company succeeded by acquiring direct rule over the Northern Cirars which are now called the coastal districts. A few years, later, the Nizam "Ceded" the districts of Bellary,Anantpur, Cuddapah,Chittor and Kurnool to the British as he could not pay for the maintenance of the of the Company's troops stationed at Hyderbad to protect him (Rao :*op.cit.*) The ceded districts were merged with the Madras Presidency under the company. The Nizam rule continued upto 1948.

In the erstwhile Nizam region (Telangana) the land was divided into three parts (1) Diwani or Khalsa area with 60% under the government land revenue system; (ii) Jagirdari system with 30% under government; and (iii) Sarf-e-khas system with 10% land under Nizam's own direct estate. The first type was akin to Ryotwari system where the landholders were not called owners *per se* but were treated as Pattadars. The actual occupants with in each Patta were called *Shikmidars* who had full rights of occupancy but were not registered. As the pressure on the land grew, the Shikmidars previously the cultivators, began to leaseout lands to subtenants (asami-shikmi) for actual cultivation. The latter were "tenants-at-will having neither rights in land nor any protection against eviction" (Alavi 1978:413). The Jagirdari system constituted the other major type of tenure system. Of the three types of tenure systems, the Sarf-e-Khas, Nizam's own direct estate or 'Crown lands' was the most obnoxious type. The income from the area amounting to Rs. 20 million annually was spent entitrely for Nizam's family and his retinue. To cap it all, the Nizam used to be given Rs. 7 million per annum from the state treasury. The peasants in the Nizam area were no more than bonded slaves.

Besides these three types of tenure systems, there were other types of *jagirs* prevalent. The *Paigas* were estates granted to Muslims as funds for supplying army to Nizam during the war. The *Jagirs* and *Samsthanams* were given to officers as rewards who served the Nizam loyally. *Maktas, banjars, agraharams* and *inams* were given to people in various services, who in turn exploited the people to the maximum. Some of them used to pay a small a portion of revenue to the state, while others were not required to pay even that much. Various types of forced labour were normal features during Nizam's region. The *Vetti* system (bonded labour) enforced the peasants and labourers to perform all sorts of household work in the land lord's house; to carry reports to police station; to keep watch on the village; supplying agricultural implements to the land lord free of cost , etc. Another type prevalent was *bhagela serfdom* where the tribal people were tied to their non-tribal masters through perpetual indebtedness (Dhanagare 1974). The *Jagirdari* system continued 1ill 1949, as a vital socio-political system. As the courts had no jurisdication over the *Jagirdars*, they were free to levy and collect taxes from the cultivators.

The *Diwani* area was under the domination of *deshmukhs* and *despandes*, who were earlier tax collectors for the government. But later during Slar Jung diwanship these collectors were granted *vatans* (annuities). Due to easy access to the landlords these *deshpandes* and *deshmukhs*, grabbed thousands of acres of fertile cultivable land fraudulently by reducing the peasants to tenants-at will or even to landless labourers (Sundariah : 1972). Usury flourished throughout the region unconditionally.

Thus the then existing hard core social conditions were the basic foundation for the Telangana insurgencies, when people felt the yoke of exploitation and the consciousness of their position took lead there upon.

The Andhra Maha Sabha established to revitalize Telugu language and culture in the erstwhile Nizam area did not have political platform in the beginning. Of course, it gained latter, but mostly for the interests of land and rich peasants and this group broke into two sections, the right wing and the left wing. The Andhra Maha Sangham with the communist ideology gathered base in rural areas and in July 1946, over 1,000 peasants went in a procession to attack a big landowner in Nalgonda district. During the attack one of the people's leaders was killed and this inspired the peasants insurrection (*ibid.*: 130) Bullets were pierced through the people; Doddi Komariah, a young leader of the march was killed and this rose the indignation of the people. The people surrounded in such a manner, that no one could come out or enter. People from the neighbouring villages came like a torrent to support the cause of people. Deshmukh Ramachandra Reddy (big landowner) sent nearly two hundred persons armed with swords and daggers to whom the irrate people gave a good push and drove them for away. The people of Kandavendi (the village of *deskmukh*) practiced social boycotts of the landlord and as a result his agriculture came to a stand still. (Reddy; 973:42).

The zamindari system or permanent settlement of estates was introduced in Andhra area as early as in 1802 and was abolished in 1949 and Ryotwari system was replaced. The *zamindari* had no occupancy rights; he being the assignee of the state could only collect a share of the produce of the land known as *malvaram*. In practice over the years the occupancy rights of ryots were obliterated with increasing rents actually being collected by the zamindars from time to time. The total *zamindari* area in the state was approximately one third of the area of the state and mostly concentrated in the Visakhapatnam and Srikakulam districts in the north, the East and West Godawari and Krishna, Nellore and Chittoor districts respectively. The *zamindari* system is these areas lasted for nearly 150 years.

The foregoing pages brief us with the social history of Andhra Pradesh. The state has to its credit large number of peasant movements right from 17th century to the present epoch. Where there is peasant movements regarding the agrarian problem, the ruling class politics becomes confrontational. Inspite of legislation and ceiling acts, rich landowners manage to retain large chunks of land due to loopholes in the laws and due to collusion with the bureaucracy. Secondly, the improved facilities of irrigation, fertilizers and pesticides together with the institutional credit have given rise to capitalist relations in some pockets and new Kulaks maneouver the politics.

Andhra Pradesh Agricultural Worker's Union an affiliate of CPI organized a march "Cooli Dandu" in 1969 to the state legislative assembly to protest against sale and transfer of land, bonded labour , fair wages, etc. About 50,000 agricultural workers from 20 districts took part in the march. (Reddy 1977).There are about 50 lakhs of acres of cultivable waste land and forest *banjara* land in Andhra Pradesh. The state government claims to have distributed 15 lakhs of acres of land. In 1969 the struggle for *banjara* land began in the Nuzvid taluka of Krishan district and took its course to Guntur, Warangal, Khammam, Adilabad and Nellore districts. Over 60,000 agricultural workers and peasants participated and more than 10,000 workers courted arrest (Report of the 9th Conference 1969:3). Besides, the political wing of CPI (M) with their peasant organizations began the land grab movements in 1970s, in Nellore, Khammam, Karimnagar, Nellore, East Godavari district, West Godavari district,Krishna and Guntur districts repectively. The Ryotu Coolie Sangham (Peasant Worker's Association), an affiliate of CPI (ML) waged struggle against land lord's tyrrany in coastal Andhra by collaboration with Radical Yuvajana Sangham and Rytu Mahila Sangham (CPI-ML Wings). It may be mentioned here that the peasant movements in Andhra Pradesh were organized by the leftist parties only. Surprisingly neither Congress nor BJP do not have any recognized and specific organization till now.

Total cultivated area according to agricultural census in 2001 was 13586 thousand hectares; out of which 954 thousand hectares were leased in. Notwithstanding the economists claims that cash rent tenancy is getting importance in India, crop-sharing tenancy by all means continue to grow in abundance (Vyas :1970). According to NSS data, the cash rent tenancy declined remarkably from 32.92% 10.4% while crop-sharing tenancy showed a definite increase from 36.55 to 57.84%. The different forms of tenancy in the state are as follows: fixed money 27.77%; fixed produce 15.44% share produce 34.36% and other kinds 21.73% hundred hectares respectively.

The state has 62,39,977 hectares of forest land and 10,42,238 hectares of cultivable wasteland. The net area sown is 415 (,12,69,233) and the total area sown in the state is 36% (1,26,52,037); besides there are various categories of land classified as seen from the Table 1.

Table 1

Classification of Land in Andhra Pradesh During 2001-02

(in hectares)

Type of Land	*Amount*	*Percentage*
Forests	62,39,977	22.8
Barren and uncultivated area	23,12,467	8.4
Land put to non-agricultural uses	20,87,207	7.6
Cultivable waste	10,42,238	3.8
Permanent pastures and grazing lands	10,28,119	3.7
Lands and under miscellaneous	2,73,771	1.0
Current fallows	23,32,338	3.1
Other fallows	8,54,709	3.1
Net Area Sown	1,12,69,233	41.0
Area sown more than once	13,82,804	5.0
Total area sown	1,26,52,037	46.0

Source: Season and crop reports of 2001-02. Bureau of Economics and Statistics, Govt. of Andhra Pradesh.

The total non-irrigated area in Andhra Pradesh is 1,09,45,937 hectares (76.12%) while the total irrigated area is 34,33,677 (23.88%) respectively (Table 2). Canals and tanks irrigate major chunk of the land i.e. 46.72%. Only 3.46% (1,19,004 hectares) of land is irrigated by tube wells. If we break up regionwise in the state,the highest percentage of non-irrigated area comes from Rayalaseema and Telangana regions (85.93% and 85.02%), while the highest percentage of irrigated land comes from coastal region (44.16%); most of the land in

Table 2
Land Irrigated and Non-Irrigated During 2001-02 in Andhra Pradesh

in hectares

Region	*Total Areas*	*Total Area Non-Irrigated*	*Total Area Irrigated*	*Canals*	*Tanks*	*Tubewells*	*Otherwells*	*Other Sources*
Coastal Region	44,90,625	25,07,806 (55.84%)	19,82,818 (44.16%)	12,60,637 (63.57%)	4,81,043 (24.26%)	1,11,626 (5.6%)	84,446 (4.2%)	45,067 (2.27%)
Rayalaseema Region	33,23,038	28,55,560 (85.93%)	4,67,478 (14.07%)	1,15,568 (24.72%)	1,16,264 (24.87%)	2,434 (0.52%)	1, 99,756 (42.73%)	33,453 (7.15%)
Telangana Region	65,65,951	55,82,671 (85.02%)	9,83,380 (14.98%)	2,28,116 (23.19%)	4,91,418 (49.97%)	4,941 (0.5%)	2, 20,659 (22.43%)	38,246 (3.88%)
Andhra Pradesh	1,43,79,614	1,09,45,937 (76/12%)	34,33,677 (23.88%)	16,04,321 (46.72%)	10,88,725 (31.70%)	1, 19,004 (3.46%)	5, 04,861 (14.70%)	1,16,766 (3.4%)

Source: Statistical Abstract of Andhra Pradesh,2004,Bureau of Economic and Statistics, Government of Andhra Pradesh

this region is irriagated by canals (63.57%); where as in Telangana region tanks irrigate the largest area i.e. 4,91,418 hectares (49.97%). Percentage of net sown area to reporting area during 2001-02 was 42.4; percentage of gross irrigated to gross sown area was 33.3; and the consumption of fertilizers per hectare of cropped area in 1993-94 are 30.3 kilograms respectively (Commerce : 2005:21). From the above description we get a rough picture of the levels of development of technology which in turn determines the politico-economic character of the state under given historical conditions.

With regard to tribal communities Andhra Pradesh hosts 16.58 lakhs belonging to nearly 33 different tribal communities. Most of them live in the north-east in Srikakulam district along the north-west line in Adilabad district with contiguous pockets in Mahaboobnagar, Kurnool and Prakasam districts. Besides there are Yerukala, Yenadi, and Sugali communities living in plain areas of coastal and Rayalaseem districts; they eke out their livelihood from collection, gathering and begging.

The industrial sector of Andhra Pradesh is moving slowly though the state has high potential. In total there are about 249 large medium scale industries in the state; as per the cottage industries there are approximately 600,000 different units. Major industries are Hindustan Shipyard; Hindustan Machines Tools, Praga Tools Corporation, The Synthetic Drug Plant at Visakhapatnam ; Singareni Collieris Company Ltd., in Khammam district; The Sirpur Paper Mills at Sirpur ; Andhra Pradesh Paper Mills at Rajamundry; A.C. Cement Factory at Vijayawada,etc. India ranks 11th in cement production in the world, and the state ranks second in the country next to Bihar and Tamilnadu. Coal accounts for about 80% of the total value of the mineral production in the state; while other major minerals are lime stone, mica and manganese. Regarding the production of agricultural implements Andhra Pradesh produces 5,000 agricultural tractors and tillers annually. Regarding the total value of out put in the manufacture of electrical machinery, apparatus and appliances, the state produced 1,88,463 lakhs of items during 1996-97 (Annual Survey of Industries 1996-97).

Even the accelerated growth witnesses since mid-1970s, the share of manufacturing in state domestic product, which was about 8% in 1960-61 increased only to 13% in 1985-86 and in 1991-1992 increased to 16.6% and 19.2% in 2006-2007. Observation from the recent experience reveal that the industrial progress in the state is not only moving towards integration with the national markets but also increasingly attracting the surpluses from the pockets of agriculturally prosperous areas of the state. Since recently India has opened the gates for the international market particularly with the multinational companies. This trend also indicates the growing capital intensity with very limited hope for any expansion of employment opportunities in the manufacturing sector. The state has a capacity to produce 6110 M.W. power; there are 565 major companies which are having the capacity in the State to employ 8.5 lakh skilled workers per a year. Since the then Telugu Desam's Government the state has become an international attraction particularly with regard to technological information system, and efforts are on to project Andhra Pradesh a model State. Accordingly, vision 2020 for the State envisages a growth of 9% to 10% .Hyderabad has come to be rendered to as Cyberabad today. Meanwhile the demand for separate Telangana state has taken the state 10 years back with a loss of several thousands of crores in 2009.

High priority was accorded to irrigation in successive five year plans by allocating 25% to 36% of State's plan outlay, with major and medium irrigation schemes receiving 85% of the public investment. Between 1959-60 and 2005-06, the total plan and non-plan public expenditure on major and medium irrigation of food grains in the state amounted to Rs. 1436 crores. Now almost every year the Irrigation Department is given huge amounts of investment during 1991-92, 1992-93,1993-94 and 2005-06, amounting to Rs. 4432 crores , Rs.4905 crores, Rs. 5206 crores and Rs. 7495 crores respectively (Statistical Outline of India,2007-08).

The result of this unequal distribution of public investment could be seen in terms of accentuated regional disparities. First , the major and medium irrigation benefits were confined to

25% of the rural population and within it pertains mostly to the landowning class. Secondly the low priority accorded to minor irrigation actually led to decline in the area under tank irrigation by almost half in the drought prone areas. The manifestations of the iniquitous public investment inirrigation could be seen clearly into divergences in productivity, employment, wages, consumption, expenditure and in a word development itself between the irrigated and drought prone areas. For instance the state has a widely diversified farming base with a rich variety of cash crops. It is surplus in food grains, produces 10 milions tons of rice and can rightly claim to be the granary of the South. Agricultural sector accounts for around 50% of the state's income and provides livelihood for 70% of the population.

According to the statistical outline of India 2004-05, the total number of agricultural labourers are 73.8% (males 45.5% ; females 28.3%). The wage rates and the per capita expenditure levels of all size class of cultivators are higher in the canal irrigated zone as compared to the dry region and the extent of difference increases with the size of the holdings. Subsequently per capita expenditure levels of small farm households in the irrigated zone exceed those of medium and large farm households in the dry zone. Thus we have over ten decades of planned development resulting in the accentuation of disparities in between the underdeveloped and developed while the share of agriculture in the state domestic product decreased from 59% to 41% and there was hardly any change in the workforce which remained around 70%. Though there has been a decline in the proposition of rural workers to total workers from 87.90% to 83.22% , the decline is much slower than the share of rural population which was 75.27% in 1961 compared to 82.56% in 1961. In 2001-02 the total workers were 52.6% in comparison with others, it increased to greater extent. An important aspect of change in the workforce refers to that of increase in the proportion of agricultural labour households in the total workforce. The rural agricultural labour pattern shows an increase in the proportion of rural agricultural labour households from 31.42% in 1964-65 to 54.6% in 2001. These trends indicate the process of proletarianisation in rural Andhra Pradesh.

In the last 60 years, the state has not achieved the national level economic development index. It has the largest share of agricultural workers compared to other states as 61% male and 83% female workers are engaged in the agricultural sector. About 39% male workers and 17% female workers are in organized sector while regular salaried employment is concentrated in urban areas.Most of the workers in rural areas are casual agricultural labourers and work participation rates for both the sexes are higher in rural areas while the urban work force is 80% and 20% for males and females. The ratio of males to females in the casual workforce is 1:7. The rural-to-urban distribution of the work force reflects a ration of 82.7:18.3. It needs to be mentioned that Andhra Pradesh has the highest work participation rates for total population and specially for its female population. While male work participation rates are higher in rural and backward areas (Sinha 1987 :419). About 80% of agriculture work is done by women. During the agricultural season women's work day spans about 15 hours. Female and child farm labour is supplied mostly from the lowest rung of the rural strata.

The process becomes sharper if we take into account the regional disparities. According to the survey of the labour force participation in backward and developed regions of the state the characteristics of labour force show clear regional differences. The occupational distribution of rural households and population constitute the single largest group in all regions. However the proportion of agricultural labour households are much higher (46.86%) in the developed regions compared to backward region (42.63%). Similarly the proportion of population of agricultural labour households is higher in developed regions (43.65%) compared to the backward region (37.74%; Table 3). The table shows that among the rural agricultural labour households the proportion of scheduled caste and scheduled tribes is much higher in developed region, 82.71% and 67.50% compared to the backward region with 70.71% and 33.93% respectively.

Table 3
Characteristics of Agricultural Labour Households in the Backward and Developed Regions of Rural Andhra Pradesh

Characteristics	*Agricultural Labour Household in*	
	Backward Region	*Developed Region*
Percentage of Scheduled Castes	70.71	82.32
Percentage of Scheduled Tribes	33.93	67.50
Proportion of landless	61.35	87.14
Average size of land owned	0.85	0.24
Average size of land cultivated (Acres)	0.81	0.14
Average Size of household	4.55	3.82
Percentage of children aged 5-9 attending school	22.57	39.66
Percentage of children aged 10-14 attending school	20.28	34.08

Sources: Census of Andhra Pradesh, 2001 Government of Andhra Pradesh, Hyderabad.

Further, among the rural agricultural labour the proportion of the landless is more as the average land owned and the average area cultivated is much less. These characteristics show that agricultural labour in the developed regions depend more on the earnings from wage labour than from their cultivation. In the same direction more industrial wage labour with better wages and relatively higher land prices is prevalent in the developed region in contrast to the backward. The smaller size of the households indicate an early formation of families due to better opportunities for independent livelihood. These regional differences are the characteristics of rural labour households are clearly reflected in their level of living condition. The proportion of the households below poverty line among the rural labour households of backward districts was of the order of 67 to 86 per cent where as the same for the developed regions ranged between 40 to 45 percent suggest the levels of uneven development pattern in the State.

After this brief background note of Andhra Pradesh we will be analyzing the field data i.e., the female workers who moved to Surat from Andhra through male migration and the subsequent processes of labour dynamics in industrial capitalism in the following chapter.

3

Women, Labour and Inequality : Empirical Findings

Despite structural differences between and among north and south countries some commonalities surface with regard to women. Largely they are relegated to procreation and rearing children particularly male children, caring the sick and old to household management, maintaining kinship relations, etc. These works are not recognized as in the case of production of goods. We may term these activities as production of services. Thus the feminist critique begins that production of goods require to proceed the production and distribution has to be people oriented, just not merely commercialized, to the enhancement of human caliber and to their refinement resulting in long term sustained development-sustenance of human kind. Needless to mention that the development models have to emphasise that the quality of the people over quantity of things which would give greater social value to the activities of women, ensuring greater freedom and value for both men and women at large.

Various micro-studies indicate that mostly women do not have access not only to economic resources but also information. The latter depends on the level of literacy mainly. For education empowers knowledge and knowledge in turn empowers awareness and strengthens the power to struggle both at home and work place and also access to paid work.

Thus the women workers in our sample numbering 220 (44%) are illiterates as per the table given below speaks the gravity of the problem.

Table 1
Level of Literacy of the Respondents

Education	*Number*	*Percentage*
Illiterate	220	44
Literate	100	20
Upto 3rd-5th standard	90	18
5th-8th standard	70	14
Upto 10th standard	20	4
Total	500	100

Simultaneously the table shows an interesting future as 280 (56%) female workers have some kind of education ranging from mere literate level to secondary education. In this context it was revealed through qualitative information that due to marriage and economic conditions besides the negligence of girl child with regard to education they could not pursue further. It may be noted here that the marriage for girls starts soon after attaining puberty i.e., between 13-14 years of age and after the marriage school is out of question as she is geared to do domestic works. There are 450 married and 50 unmarried women in our sample. Despite the inherent obstacles in the system the significant positive factor with regard to relatively high literacy level in the sample is perhaps due to the prevalence of left movement in the native region (Telangana districts , A.P.) of the respondents which gets reflected at the wider level. For instance women are the cultivators and yet they are not recognized as land titles are granted to men only (Stand 1976). Further the concerned studies also point out that in most of the households women are the bread-winners. It is estimated that 15%-25% of households in third world countries are headed by women; 20% in the Caribbean and Central America; 22% in sub-Saharan Africa; 16% in North Africa and the Middle East; 15% in South America and 18.7% in India (Buvinic and Yousseff, 1978). Some research on women in West

Africa observe that women besides as wage labourers, petty traders, farm workers, etc. also work in the "household units" of production comprising family labour under the male management (Roberts,1989). Women are subordinated in the production and distribution of goods within the household do not receive proposed share of benefits with the household ironically to which they themselves have contributed.

By and large in third world societies age and sex constitute as the prime categories of the division of labour which enforces the interdependence of family labour and this type of division of labour is legitimized and is perpetuated by a specific set of norms resulting in gender identities. The gender based works incorporates cultural assessment of their social value, legitimizing the unequal distribution of the products of labour in the household (*ibid*). In this connection the debated issue i.e., the women in development in the third world is invariably related to the role of multinationals and the nature of female participation in the work force. Notwithstanding the female participation in the labour market due to the penetration of foreign capital into the third world countries, it also created new forms of subordination.

In social sciences particularly in anthropology and sociology there exists invisibility of women either deliberately or otherwise in history and society. Origin and development of sexism has been kept unanswered by the concerned social scientists and at times though written the women's voice has been mute (Reiter, 1975;Rosaldo and Lamphere, 1974). By and large kinship and family studies portray women as merely assisting beings in the social structure. It may also be mentioned in this context that women's concerns in social studies has been equally neglected by a large number of female sociologists and anthropologists. Mostly anthropology as a whole pictured male view of third world societies. While some developed theories like "humankind minus women" or reduced women to mere cogs in social hierarchy (Tiger, 1970). More often than not anthropologists have not dealt the women's problem seriously besides portraying a kind of male reality equivalent to the whole group as if, thereby reducing women as mere appendages. Yet no concerned academic could cross the bridge without provoking professional commitment (Ardener, 1972). In defence they thus argue that women are not taken as a unit of scientifically characterised, rather they are as if an ideological unit (Leeds, 1976). Accordingly it is increasingly felt that many ethnographic documents need to be re-written which were produced particularly under colonialism (Hymes, 1972; Ma-feje.1071; Davis, 1973). In this connection some researchers observe that women are in accessible. Perhaps this could be partly due to prevailing traditions and partly due to researcher's assumption that men informed better (Elkan, 1956).

Be that as it may that it is a truism that social anthropology has a reputation for its ever lasting interest and therefore specialization in the sexual practices of exotic peoples. In the 19th century anthropology studied sex and gender; marriage; family and sexual roles were assumed until about 1860 belonging to the natural conditions of humanity. However it was felt that family of the Victorian middle class was not the result of the operation of natural laws, but of a long and painful evolutionary struggle. Accordingly sexuality was identified with animality and thus "savages" were equated with nature and the sexual habits of primitive peoples were seen as more animalistic than their own. Many anthropologists opined that the struggle against sexual instincts as the earliest triumph of 'man' against nature. Towards the end of the century were linked with social Darwinsm in the Spencerian analyses to arrive at the rigidly defined sex roles with male domination and suppression of female sexuality stating that these were not historical but adaptations to social survival. By the early 20th century anthropology had to reckon with Freudian psychoanalysis. Anthropologists challenged the Freudian notions of Oedipus complex by mentioning that it does not exists specially in the matrilineal societies (Malinowksi,1927). However Malinowski had Adam-Eve assumptions about the nature of women and sexual relations by upholding marriage in all societies as sacrament. On the whole though anthropologists studied the institution of marriage, family and social structures, little was attempted to theorise sexuality, surely not gender, because anthropology viewed people in genral and women in particular as objects than subjects in the process of social transformation.

Meanwhile Mead's research in Samoa left a considerable influence upon theories of gender and sexuality where she observes that gender is a socially constructed phenomenon rather than biological and most importantly she argued that sexuality is not repressed alike in all cultures uniformly as assumed in the west (Mead, 1928; 1935). None the less issues like kinship, marriage, incest, family, etc. were not directly and emphatically addressed in anthropology as anthropologists shied away from the political and practical implications of work (Coward, 1983). But the studies on symbolism forced anthropologists to analyse sexuality indirectly (Bateron, 1958; Gough, 1955, Richards, 1982; Turner, 1967; 1968). Besides another area of symbolism dealing with sexuality is the study of human body (Hertz, 1960; Leach, 1958; Douglas,1960; 1970). Mention may be made that many studies observed that the bodies of women are made to serve as social symbols (Yalman, 1963; Fruzzetti, 1982; Bennett, 1982; Kenney, 1970; Hosken, 1976, Saadwi, 1980).

Extrapolating from the findings we argue that the family is used to reproduce and socialise labour while the wages are used for family's needs in turn. Under precapitalism social and economics function as a single unit mostly, keeping household as a major unit of productive organization, thus strengthening the family's hold. As we notice from our data that women enter in paid employment since in unorganised sector male wages are not enough to ensure the survival which necessitates the pooling of resources from the other family members to support the household economy. In this connection we also observed that by the nature of better wages male dominate in the family with low wages make them subordinated although if counted unpaid domestic labour, besides biological reproduction female work participation by far exceeds enormously (Table 2).

Table 2
Distribution of Female Work Force in the Sample

Work Category	*Number of Workers*	*% of Worker*	*Work Hazards*
Home-based production (paid labour + domestic work*) jari work, making plastic bags, lace bags and bidi rolling	330	66	Poor Eye sight Back Pain + Stress and strain
Market production (paid labour +domestic work* winding (textiles)	150	30	Back pain + Strain
Only Domestic work* (unpaid labour) Cooking,cleaning,washing,fetching water, rationing from PDS,nursing the sick,etc.	20	04	Back pain + Strain
Total	500	100	

There is a marked sexual division of labour like, 'men's job' and 'women's job' within the family and this process is reproduced outside in the labour market, be it industrial or agricultural. For instance largely only women transplant, harvest, weeding, pounding, husking, bidi rolling, making home based foods like wafers, 'papad', lace making, jari works, etc. all consume umpteen hours of drudgery at the cost of their health. All these works reflect on women's –well being of the individual causing physical and psychological imbalances. Secondly this rigid division of labour leaves a formidable strain on women causing back-pain and related diseases.The table reveals that 66% of the female work force from the sample suffer from severe back-pain, dwindling eye sight, mental and physical strain besides other routine health disorders like cold and fever,headache,jaundice,gastro-enteritis, anaemia and so on not only due to improper imbalance of food intake but also because of their own negligence of their health due to lack of time and long hours of work. Meanwhile it is a fact that by and large all women particularly in the third world countries neglect their own health and other personal concerns vis-à-vis the rest in the family. Perhaps this may be due to the very socialization process of women, that "others first than self" and secondly , due to strong hold of pre-capitalist relations of production. In this connection it may be mentioned that domestic work by and large has four attached assumptions dividing both the sexes; (i) economic dependence through a marriage a common stereotype; (ii) exclusive allocation of work to women; (iii) it's subsequent status as unproductive work; and (iv) primacy to women only i.e., priority over other roles (Oakley, 1974). Accordingly domestic work carries cultural and social dimension that it is assumed of having sacrificial and pleasure dimension socially and survival culturally (Beston, 1969). By the very notion the domestic work stands in violent contrast to the rest of the occupations (Caplan, 1954).

Mention may be made that in pre-capitalist social formations there is no sharp distinction between work and leisure. Activities are carried out in terms of interpersonal relations and social roles rather than pure economism. Among foraging communities hunting, planting, tool making, cooking etc. were considered both as leisure and work as well. It is however with the penetration of capitalism housework ceases to be nonwork. The wage labour is sustained by socially necessary but private labour of wives, sisters and mothers. Historically it is contended that the modern family is the recent creation of the industrialization process. The male supremacy became institutionalised in the capitalist system of production and thus "while housewives and mothers continued their traditional task of production-housework, child-rearing, etc.- their labour was devalued through its isolation through its isolation from production–housework, child rearing, etc.-their labour was devalued through its isolation from production of surplus value. Besides "housewives and mothers were given new responsibility for maintaining the emotional psychological realm of personal relations" (Zaretsky, 1976:31). The syllogism that "a housewife is a woman and what she does it not work" and is institutionalised in women.

It is assumption that man is the breadwinner and head of the family as women are naturally best adapted for mothering and nurturing the children and the husband. In other words this is regarded as a "natural" divsdion of labour in the family. In order to comprehend the sexual division of labour it is essential to browse the connotation of family in capitalism and within this matrix the domestic labour respectively in the following. At the outset it is a fact that with regard to family and capitalism by and large the trend has been either economic reductionism or over emphasis of family as an ideological institution (Creighton, 1985). Nevertheless the domestic labour debate particularly in Marxist analyses, family under capitalism needs to be analysed on material basis and the socialisation of children as a main point to the maintenance of capitalist relations.

The dominant concept in the works of Marx and Engels is that of property relations and extended this critique to family relations within capitalist society by observing that how love is replaced by economic criterion by supplementing the mechanical relations through prostitution. However Engels in the *Origin of Private Property, Family and State*, tries to offer a systematic analysis of the family. Adopting historical method he analysed the relating changes in the form of marriage in pre-class society and the transition to class society, following the changes in forces and social relations of production. In the earliest phase of social development descent was traced through the female line, marriage could be easily dissolved, women and supremacy in the household and household labour had not got separated from social production. There was a strict division of labour between the sexes, however not much inequality was found between them. In later course these relations were altered by new economic and social forces, specially by the domestication of animals which led to concentration of wealth and its resources in males privately. Eventually, the passing of wealth to their own children led men to replace female by male descent and concomitant urge to ensure strictly their heirs resulted in the formation of monogamous family and subsequently male supremacy. In due course these changes institutionalised female subordination and brought it radical shifts in the family. Therefore Engels argued that the privatisation of domestic was one of the chief obstacles in the emancipation of women (Engels, 1972 : 282).

In this connection many Marxist scholars particularly the western counterparts began their analysis from this starting point i.e., domestic labour as central issue. They argue that in economic terms domestic labour in capitalism replenishes the task of labour-power and opine that domestic labour contributes directly or indirectly to surplus value.[1]

We opine that domestic labour debate poses theoretical, methodological and substantive weakness and thus there is a need to re-examine the concept under capitalism. Domestic labour either produces surplus value directly or creates value which is embodied in labour power and is felt when the later is exchanged (Secombe, 1974). We argue that both the statements are based on the assumption that domestic labour can be viewed as abstract labour. But this equation does not hold firm since domestic labour is privatized producing only use values and secondly it is also felt that it is not part of social production and therefore carried on independently of the law of value (Gardiner, 1975; Fee, 1976). Further this view holds that domestic labour contributes to surplus value by keeping the level of wages below the value of labour power. Contradicting this others have convincingly argued that the relationship between the domestic labour and the value of labour power is not an invariant one and therefore must be established empirically (Molyneux, 1979; Breugel, 1978). While in certain conditions domestic labour may not be the cheapest way of meeting worker's needs and this on the contrary might be the common situation historically given that the cost of supporting a full-time housewife has to be covered by paying men a "family wage". Further it conflates with the reproduction and to conflate the question of the effect of labour power upon surplus value with the issue as to why that housework is only allotted very convincingly to women (Fee, *Op.cit.*). Still others hold that the sexual division of labour within the family is dependent on the existence of family household (Creighton, 1985).

Meanwhile methodologically the domestic labour debate is based on functionalist notion that it is functionally necessary for capital. Thus this assumption observes the working of capital in relation to the family. Despite the necessity of family for capitalism it undermines family in focusing contradictions between family and capital (Breugel, 1978). Further functionalism fails to explain how family stands in opposition to capitalism (Caulifield, 1974; Humphires, 1977). A significant methodological problematique is the economic reductionism in domestic labour issue which marginalizes the ideological dimension of the family and the interaction of family with the social relations of capitalism. It also assumes that the family is not safe at economic level, and so depends on state and other agencies for its survival (Mckintosh, 1978). Besides domestic labour debate's narrow focus upon surplus value does not exhaust other economic dimensions, as there are numerous forms of labour processes and labour market. In this connection Blumenfeld and Mann (1980) hold that "there is also a qualitative and inalienable aspect of child-rearing which is part of the process of becoming human, even within capitalist society, where the process is distorted " (p.296). The needs and their satisfaction are better understood within the context of specific of social formation.

From this framework we note that material production has two aspects ; (i) the production of the means of subsistence; and (ii) the human production which is associated with the family. However reproduction is not homogeneous a there is distinct human (biological) reproduction, the reproduction of labour force and social reproduction (Edholm, *et.al.*,1977). Meanwhile we cannot equate the relations of production with patriarchy or with the sex-gender system as these relations are equally imposed on men by other men as well, like on women. In other words the mechanics of social controls operate through various media i.e., class, state, culture, traditions, etc., and affect both men and women equally (Forster and Ranum, 1976). The economic activities of the family i.e., the nature of the family as economic, political and cultural unit, the significance of demostic labour and its relations with the sexual division of labour and the affects of socilaisation for economic, political and cultural unit, the significance of domestic labour and its relation with the sexual division of labour and the effects of socialization for economic, political and other processes of capitalist society are missing in domestic theory. Argued simply that family is not an autonomous institution. Therefore it is erroneous to presume that family household exists due to the interests of capitalism and thus cannot be analysed from economic and ideological requirements of capitalism. All said capitalism is unable to generate an alternate institution to family. At all levels the interests of capitalism contradict between capitalists and the workers seems to be an unrealistic conjecture; rather they over lap at times and here the maintenance of family is one such area.

The Table reveals the co-existence of paid labour and unpaid labour in the household unit in capitalism which in turn reflects the social relations and production and reproduction and how it is being reproduced. Besides it also

Table 3
Wages, Economic Participation and Allocation of Time

Work	*Wages in Rs.P/D*	*Nature of Production*	*Time in hrs.*
Jari work + DW	15	Home based	3-5 + 5 dw
Winding + DW	35-50	Factory based	8 + 5 dw
Making of plastic and lace bags, bidis , etc. + DW	15-20	Home based	3-5+5 DW
Only domestic work	Unpaid labour	Home based without exchange value	7-9

Note: DW denotes domestic work (unpaid labour).

implies, the existence of unorganized and that too female work force with cheap production cost for the advantage of capitalism, as all the economic activities excluding winding job in the sample take place at home. During the fieldwork we noticed that there is no leisure time for the women workers who are with home-based production which means only work all day. This necessarily means low wages, unspecified long hours and tedious work in tandem with unending domestic drudgery for women. In this context we argue that the unpaid domestic labour of women generates the paid labour force (both men and women) that is necessary for the maintenance of capitalism. Our data also show that on an average woman more work more than ten hours per day. It needs to be mentioned that several qualitative tasks performed by them could not be quantified.If we include these works on crude estimates the number of work hours would go beyond 15 hour schedule per day. The analysis of labour supply to the market by way of theory of demand for leisure time and hours of work in the market constitute an exhaustive dichotomy. Accordingly the logical compliment to leisure time is work broadly construed, whether it includes remunerative production in the market or work that is currently unpaid. The latter includes various forms of investment oneself, the production of goods and services for home and family. Work at home is an activity to which women on an average devote the larger part of their married life and thus it becomes an exclusive work of many women. We observed in our study that the total amount of work performed both at home and outside is an outcome of family demand. Meanwhile we noticed that increased family income does not mean decrease of total hours of work at home.

Throughout history the amount of time spent at work has never constantly been much grater than that spent on other activities. In this regard allocation and non-working times becomes crucial to economic welfare than that of working time (Becker, 1965). It is essential to treat indirect costs on the same footing while discussing non-work uses of time. Therefore we submit that it is not only difficult to distinguish leisure from non-work but also even work from non-work. Further our data reveal that the women in the sample spend equal time in domestic work as in paid work (Table 3.) Where as middle class and upper middle class women spend less time on domestic work as these tasks would be performed by the female hired-in labour belonging to marginalized section of the society, i.e., women appropriating women's labour.

It may be noted that private property exists in almost all modes of production, but its form, extent and implications differ according to the dominant mode of production. Monogamy is neither necessary nor a sufficient condition for the existence of family. The family has social relations network that needs to be produced and sustained by said practices reinforcing reciprocal kinship relations, as kinship ties rest on material base. Family provides services and stability to capital on one side and on the other controls and oppresses women through patriarchy. However it is equally important to cognize that family also provides to an extent emotional support and security to its members (both men and women), while it reduces when women get married. However it may be stressed here that the family support system operates on unequal relations between men and women.

In the fitness of things it is worth to comprehend Marx's analysis of working class family in *Capital* as the reproduction of labour power. Accordingly Marx holds that firstly, the proletarian family is the centre of production; purchase goods (input) with the family wages and in turn renews labour power which is sold for wages (output) in the market. In short household activity of the working class family is tailored to capitalist mode of production through the reproduction of labour power cycle as he observes that "the maintenance and reproduction of the working class is and must ever be , a necessary condition to the reproduction of capital" (Marx, 1967 :572). Therefore at the level of abstraction the issue of domestic labour is crucial to understand the relationship between women's oppression and capitalism. Secondly, Marx goes on to state that it is the sensibility of value of labour power to the employment structure of the working class family. Thus he writes: "There are, besides, two other factors that enter into the determination of the value of labour power. One the expenses of developing that labour power, which expenses vary with the mode of production; the other, its natural diversity, the difference between the labour power of men and women, of children and adults" (*ibid.*:519). Marx stressed the increase of working women and children which he held as universal proletarianization and the increase of value of labour power in the working class family. Though Marx does not pursue this argument further, the decrease of value of labour power in the family due to universal proletarianization, enables the working class to defend the traditional family structure.

Table 4
Bifurcation of Domestic Work

Work	*Approximate Time (in hours)*
Cooking	1
Cleaning (sweeping, mopping and washing utensils)	1 1/2
Washing clothes	1 1/2
Fetching Water	1 1/2
Fetching rations from PDS (Fair Price Shop)	2 1/2
Child care and nursing the sick*	Varies and unlimited as the work involved is qualitative
Total	8(excluding*)

Regardless of the differences on the question of domestic labour there are some important concerns where we can come to an agreement. Often it is assumed that the payment made by capital to labour is based on the existence of certain value of domestic work and state services. The influence of capital is such that in the presence of domestic labour, the wage is lower than it would have been; if the working class family would depend on purchased commodities. Thus the surplus labour is extracted from the domestic work and ultimately transformed into surplus value (Humphries 1980). However we should not over generalize the role of capital exclusively without relations of production and class antagonisms theoretically or else we would trip on technological determinism. The Tables 4 and 5 pointout the bifurcation of different essential household activities that are necessary for daily survival and maintenance of the family. We wish to state clearly that unpaid labour tasks are exclusively performed by women largely. The time required for each work only shows approximation and this we deduced through umpteen informal tasks, observations and through cross-checking during data collection. None the less we admit the apparent arbitrariness in calculating time due to the sensitive nature of work, internalization process and the limitation of time from the respondents. Secondly we did not include child care and nursing the sick, exclusively personal works related to health, aesthetics, leisure and other activities which are qualitative in nature and certainly cannot be quantified mechanistically. We see from the Table 4 that though all women work in all types, the major tasks have been cooking (95%) followed by the most tedious job of getting rations (80%) particularly kerosene oil, sugar and rice. More often the women have to stand in long queus irrespective of weather only in vain, as the shopkeeper does not give proper time. Besides he carries the ration distribution slowly and often many women after standing several hours have to return with empty cans with bitter feelings. During this standing session they exchange and share their concerns, pains and pleasures on several issues ranging from dowry related murders particularly among the Telugu migrants besides various forms of prevalent domestic violence, the conflicts in the household, the happenings in their native place and so on to other issues like movies, festival operations, chit fund activities, buying ornaments or consumer items etc. Furthermore we also noticed that the labour-intensive but cheap production-cost work based on home production (66%) exploit female work force as the readily available cheap organised labour gets integrated to the capitalist market locally and globally. At the face of it the most labour intensive and time and health consuming domestic work does not seem to have exchange value directly. However, it enters indirectly through the relations of reproduction. Meanwhile it is worth to note the role of homebased production which is threefold: (1) restriction of women's mobility, a sort of sergregation at work, (2) increase in the rate of domestic work almost without any time for self and above all resulting in deterioration of women's health; and (3) finally, inducing in the minds that it is not an important economic activity and creating and enhancing notion of dependency on the male. Precisely as many as 66% of the women interviewed are engaged in this poorly paid home based economic activity stated that they 'do not work' but perform only housework. Besides this "only house work" is so internalized by the women that they do not consider work at all and on the contrary they see it as a part of womanhood. Ergo home based production not only strengthens patriarchy but also reinforces on the one hand and integrates these home based female workers to capitalist mode on the other. This clearly specifies that patriarchy is not autonomous as some would make us think.

It is a fact that some labour is necessary to safeguard the survival of the family to which the individual belongs as Marx aptly calls as "the ensemble of the social relations" (Marx 1967:7). Accordingly it implies that labour has to relate to the maintenance and reproduction of the individual in certain definite relationships. This requires some surplus labour over and above necessary labour, which is present in all modes of production. This way domestic labour has use values encompassing the socially necessary labour time to secure the conditions of reproduction in all social formations. But in capitalism the domestic labour becomes isolated and this separation renders it invisible and value-less. Thus the unequal relations between men and women reinforce the differences between sexual division of labour in the market. And therefore the productivity of wage labour rises in relative terms with the domestic work by strengthening the unequal relations among the skilled and semi-skilled workers which is further pushed by the domestic work (Humphries 1980). While in pre-capitalist economic formations all the family members ensure subsistence of the family unit whereas in the capitalist mode of production the survival conditions make this process difficult as the direct producer is separated from the means of production and is appropriated of their surplus labour in the form of surplus value. Therefore proletarianization of some family members become imperative for survival. As is evident from the Tables 4 and 5, both wage workers and domestic workers participate in the exchange of activities and services. As mentioned domestic labour is separated from the means of exchange and therefore becomes invisible and distinct from the wage work. By the way relations of dominance and subordination pertaining to age and sex division of labour exist within the family. This by no means denote either glorification or idealization of family.

Accordingly age and sex as prime categories of division of labour particularly in the third world societies enforces the dependence of family labour and gets legitimised. This process is continually perpetuated by a specific set of norms which in turn ensure gender identity. The gender based works like cooking, cleaning, washing, child care, etc. incorporates cultural assessment of their social value resulting in legitimisation of unequal distribution of the products of labour in the household.

The table points out that even in paid labour category direct market related labour has favorable exchange value than than those enter the labour via, households. Thus 80 workers earn between 1000-1200 per month while 55 of them earn ranging from Rs. 600-1000 respectively proves the market value of the labour. On the contrary the home-based worker's earnings start from only Rs.400 and reach below Rs.800 per month. Only

Table 5
Exchange of Labour in the Market (P/M)

Wages in Rs.	*Work*					
	Winding	%	*Jari Works*	%	*Making Bags & Bidis*	%
400-600	k	k	40	22.22	80	53.33
600-800	20	13.33	120	66.67	60	40
800-1000	35	23.33	20	11.11	10	6.67
1000-1200	80	53.33	k	k	k	k
1200-1400	15	10	k	k	k	k
>1400	k	k	k	k	k	k
Total	150	100	180	100	150	100

Note: Out of 500 sample 20 repondents perform only domestic work which cannot be exchanged in themarket.

about 30 workers manage to earn between Rs.800-1000 rarely. We reiterate that these home-based works are not only labour intensive but also time consuming. The complex part of these works is their adjustment or combining with the domestic work as more often women jointly perform both at the same time. For instance while cooking or waiting to fetch water or standing in the queue for ration before the public distribution shop they do lace works and other related works which have exchange value. So we argue that money value for the paid work is derived from the time value of the unpaid work. Secondly we also hold that this kind of labour processes deprive the people of thinking and reflecting and divert their objectives to market direction. Both the arguments hold true for the direct market labour too. Thus,

Exchange value for Market and Home Production = Non exchange of Domestic labour + Exchange Value of Market Labour.

∴ *Paid Labour value = Unpaid Labour Time + paid Labour Time*

Accordingly, domestic labour is socially reproductive labour expended in the context of domestic unit. Hence it is essential to understand the mechanism of articulation of domestic labour with different modes of production (Caplan and Bujra, 1978). As we know modes of production are the historically conditioned specific forms found in the socio-economic formation at a given point of time. The process of production in itself constitutes reproduction more so in respect to capitalism. It is a fact that in any given mode the reproduction of labour power i.e., the renewal of the capacity or energy to labour spent in production process becomes an indispensable factor. Here lies the context of domestic labour and its articulation with the mode of production and it may be argued that domestic labour is socially reproductive as paid labour is derived from the combination of unpaid labour time and paid labour time. At the very outset it is a daily labour expended in cooking, cleaning, washing, childcare, etc. Besides through existing ideologies children are socilised in such a way as to articulate domestic labour to the relations of production.

Thus women's labour particularly in working class family serves in two ways by producing and generating socially necessary labour force and corresponding relations of capitalism. The correlation between the wage level and working class living conditions depends on purchased commodities and on household activity. For, wages have to be transformed into the use values consumed in the home, a transformation embodying a considerable time. It may be recalled once again that our sample of female workers hail from the Telugu speaking industrial labour who have migrated from Andhra Pradesh. As many as 350 respondent's either husband or father/brother (70%) own below two acres of dry land with poor remuneration while 150 (30%) do not own any agricultural land in their native place. They were supplementing their income through available agricultural labour before their migration to Surat. It may be noted here that none of the women in our sample own any land as the property ownership rights are male based largely. However widows do inherit ownership rights, but we do not have any widows in our sample.

Meanwhile, it is worth to note that the hierarchical division of labour within the family which assigned husband the role of bread-winner and wife the role of domestic caretaker emerged only in the nineteenth century as was associated with the emergence of middle class and the diffusion of its values (Aries, 1962). On the other hand the peasant families as well as working class families did not find feminine and economic functions incompatible. Rather it was held that women would work, as their contribution is necessary for the survival of family unit. The division of labour by sex appears to be almost universal in human history. In this context in-depth work is required at different class levels with regard to the redefinition of family relationships and the changes in the definition of women's work and women's place that accompanied. As mentioned earlier we reiterate that private property exists in almost all modes of production, but its form, extent and implications differ according to the dominant mode of production. The family has social relations network based on genealogical relationships that needs to be produced and sustained by social practices reinforcing reciprocal kinship relations. In this context we come across studies holding that "lines of class division and conflict run between but not through families" and that "the position of the family as a whole within the system of stratification... deprives from that of the family 'head' the separation of sex roles within the family... being itself the expression of a major form of inequality existing between the sexes" (Goldthorpe, 1983 : 468-469). Family is not an organic whole, but a hierarchical system. Kinship and parenthood are not natural but are essentially social institutions. Therefore in actuality it is not possible to analyse sexuality without relating to the political economy within which it is embedded. In other words we cannot understand sexuality as a concept without contextualizing as sexual practices do not exist in a vacuum and thus cannot escape the cultural set. Precisely as "what people want and what they are made to want and allowed to do" (Caplan, 1984:25). Sexual identities are culturally and historically specific and are relational and are about our relationships to ourselves, precarious unities of conflicting desires and social commitments "composed of heterogeneous fragments of fossilized cultures" (Gramsci, 1975 : 213). Identity is historically contigent, seemingly inevitable, potentially limiting and politically essential. To reiterate sexual identities are encoded in a complex web of social practices-legal, pedagogic and personal.

In a world of widening inequalities and injustice there is but a natural existence of unequal relations between men and women and any imagination sans inequality is next to impossible under the given conditions of political economy. We argue that gender based subordination has curtailed women's access and control to resources and labour power and imposed sexual division of labour. Women do not have control over themselves, their person, their thoughts, their actions and on their own labour power as the informal interviews of the respondents in the present exercise reveal. They need prior clearance from their husbands/fathers/brothers with regard to expenditure of their own earnings. The following Table 6 shows the pattern of expenditure in household units.

Table 6
Distribution of Wages According to Household Needs (Monthly)

Category	*Number of Respondents*	*Percentage*
Household survival	220	44
Chit fund	100	20
Clothes and Jewellery	50	10
Debt clearance	50	10
Domestic requirements (utensils and small domestic items)	40	8
Furniture	20	4
Total	500	100

We infer from the above that about fifty per cent spend their earnings on survival needs of the households like purchasing provisions, vegetables, fuel and the like. It may be recalled once again that the respondents hail from the migrant households in Surat City. These migrants work as textile labourers and the industrial units employ predominantly male migrants particularly in the weaving section. More often the spouses of the migrants supplement the survival and the other household requirements in order to meet the escalating urban cost of living. It is essential to note here that without women's work (paid) it is difficult to manage the household in urban area and therefore women's paid labour besides unpaid labour forms an important factor in the reproduction of industrial capital. Besides other family members of the migrants also work to ensure the survival of the household. It may be noted here that women migrate through marriage particularly with regard to the working class in Surat. The migrant labour comes to Surat from different states in the country like, Andhra Pradesh, Orissa, Uttar Pradesh, Bihar, Maharashtra etc. Accordingly the women respondents'economic participation in our study needs to be cognized from this background.

Secondly the textile industry is shrinking since recently resulting in closure of sick units and also reduction in work days due to frequent strikes by the owners and the workers besides regular power cuts. Thus the approximate number of paid work days would be between 20-22 days per month. Therefore women's contribution is all the more crucial for the family survival in Surat and hence we argue for equal weightage for women's labour although their earnings are at low level than the males in the family. Besides as mentioned earlier not only their paid work but also the unpaid domestic labour jointly forms an integral part of industrial capitalism. Meanwhile about hundred respondents invest on 'chitfund' through which they buy necessary items for the family like consumer goods, furniture, and also clear their debts booth in Surat and in the village. The table shows that only 50 women spend on clothes and jewellery while 450 of them (90%) spend for the maintenance of the family unit in different ways.

Our data reveal that 450 households in the sample are indebted ranging from three thousand to eighteen thousand rupees to the moneylender in the village in Andhra Pradesh (Table 7). While fifty households do not have any debts in the village and are creditors to friends and relatives in Surat. Main reasons for debt are survival and dowry as most of the respondents hail from small peasant and agricultural labouring classes. More often they mortgage small parcels of land to the village landlord-cum-moneylender. We found that one of the major factors of migration to Surat is indebtedness followed by less work opportunities, irregular and low income.

The table show that about 50% of the sample households are in debt of below five thousand rupees largely for food and social customs associated with post-marriage customs, birth and death besides sickness of relatives and friends while the maximum debt range indicates that about 31% are in debt of below twenty thousand rupees towards marriage expenses, mostly involving dowry followed by house repair or construction respectively. The data also show that only two households took loan below five thousand rupees for sending their children to college education to a nearby town, in Andhra

Table 7
Debt Pattern of the Households in the Sample

(*in Rs.*)

Reasons	*Amount*							
	<5000		*5001-10000*		*100001-20000*		*Total*	
	No.	*%*	*No.*	*%*	*No.*	*%*	*No.*	*%*
Food	150	33.33	k	k	k	k	150	33.33
Marriage	20	4.44	50	11.11	60	13.33	130	28.88
House/Repair/Construction	k	k	20	4.44	70	15.55	90	19.99
Social Obligations	50	11.11	k	k	k	k	50	11.11
Health	5	1.11	5	1.11	10	2.22	20	4.44
Others	2	0.44	8	1.77	k	k	10	2.22
Total	227	50.43	83	18.43	140	31.1	450	99.96

Pradesh while eight took loan to purchase two-wheeler (Luna) and to open a petty grocery shop in the village. Largely the continuous debt trap compels the people to migrate to industrial cities like Surat. Here it may be noted that women migrated to Surat through marriage as males migrate first and after securing regular job as weavers in the textile sector would bring their spouses to the city. And it is here women's labour needs to be cognised as her contribution is a determining factor in the production of capital. Therefore we reiterate that although women are not prime migrants as males, their participation as *indirect working class* as our data reveal is an essential feature of capitalism in third world societies. We term indirect because the women workers as in our sample are related to the production process indirectly through their unpaid domestic labour and directly through paid labour to the market while their male counterparts have direct relations of production. Precisely as chores like cleaning, cooking, washing, nurturing, etc. are generally understood to be the part and parcel of female work. Domestic work is more intertwined, insperable and invisible from the paid work in the household. Sexual division of labour within a class in the sexual divison of resources, changes in the sex resource base affects either increasing or decreasing of resources in the class (Leacock, 1979). Therefore it is necessary to understand the interrelations between production and reproduction as part of a single process and it is essential to explore relationship of family with the socio-economic and political processes under capiatalism.

After going through the empirical analyses with regard to women's labour and its implications we felt it necessary to examine the violence of women in the family in brief. There is no dearth to the plethora of existing literature, seminars and conferences held which analysed, diagnosed, counseled, prescribed or proscribed violence. Precisely as violence is a social phenomenon of a great magnitude, but often little is understood in political-economic context. Broadly speaking violence is viewed in two dimensions; (i) structural violence and the state with manifold exploitation and appropriation of one class by another while the state protects the appropriator class leading to various forms of violence; and (ii) the specific violence is which operates in the former matrix includes violence against women, children, minorities, weaker sections, etc. Violence of this nature is historically and structurally specific in corresponding socio-economic formation.

Largely speaking violence both in general and specific terms is the result of politico-economic crisis at national and international levels. Unequal distribution and exchange, unemployment, underemployment and the inflation showing stubborn resistance to all hitherto known remedies, is the prevailing social order. We argue that this economic crisis is the reflection of global crisis. And is unlikely to recover without structural changes. At this juncture it is opined that specific violence against women is the result of inevitable crumbling of social values and degradation of humanity (Pathy, 1987). Violence needs to be analysed within the broader quest for social justice, the relationship between violence and inequality i.e., unequal distribution of means of production and unequal relations between men and women. In other words violence is perceived better within the context of structural injustice, domination and subordination. The violence against women has to be understood from its political nature and content. We argue that concepts like male violence, family violence etc. relegate to private realm and finally to the individual divorced from the political economy. Existing social relations are shaped by unequal relations between men and women, and are constantly reproduced resulting in perpetual subordination of women in society. Violence is the extreme manifestation of extreme inequality, resulting in the oppression of women, which in turn serves the system in different ways. In the family, woman is a "possession" of her husband with male hierarchy and the very social fabric of male domination denies equal access to women *(ibid.)* The institution of marriage and the relations of production ensures women's subordination. Male-female relations are the prototype of relations of domination and subordination. This way violence against women emerges in the family i.e., the cradle of violence. Child abuse, wife beating, 'granny bashing' and the assault of husband, all take place quietly within the four walls of family.

More often than not the violence against women is 'suppressed' within the households as it is supposedly belongs to private realm. Thus we encountered women saying, "after all it (any form of violence) is a household matter. How can others intervene? It happens in every house" and the like. Further during the investigation we also observed that women have internalized to contain the oppression within themselves inorder to protect 'family's honour'. However the victim wishes to share in private the reason as well as mode of violence. Our qualitative data reveal that nearly all the respondents are subjected to various types of violence ranging from verbal abuse, humiliation of the person and her family (parental-if married), restricting her movements , etc., resulting in violent beating. The reasons for the violence at the outset are broadly economic and social. The former relates to the oppressive system of exploitation of working class by capitalism where the workers are alienated from the means of production. The latter reflects the unequal relations between men and women and are constantly reproduced culminating in the perpetual subordination of women in society. In other words violence is the extreme manifestation of extreme inequality which serves the system in different ways. In the family the very social fabric of male domination denies equal access to women. However we argue that transhistorical subordination of women varies according to specific historical conjunctions. For, the reproduction of labour power revolves around sexual division of labour within specific modes of production. The family reproduces relations of ideology and relations of production; because in the family property relations become the historical expression between men and women.

The regulation of female sexuality is carried with utmost social legitimacy. The informal discussions with the respondents and our observation during investigation reveal that the women have internalised social mores like to be passive, obedient and tolerant of the violence (physical and other forms like abuse and humiliation), to be stoical and bear all kinds of discrimination. It may be mentioned that the women's body invariably forms the content and form of the abuse, whether the contradiction is between men and women or between and among men. Sexual abuses are collective and receive social sanctions. Women have been the butt of male ridicule in proverbs and myths alike in insulting women's bodies, mocking their mental capacities. Thus she is not spared even in abuses! An interesting feature (not surprisingly) from the present study is that there is persistence of cultural attitudes despite the adoption of leftist ideology which fails to harmonise the relations between men and women. Secondly the subtle influence of capitalism on women is the creation and maintenance of cheap labour reserve on one side and keeping the male wage level low on the other in urban areas. We found that women do not migrate to urban area themselves and for their own progress, but move through their males only as our study points out. We also noticed that despite the accumulated work as well as tedious domestic work besides paid work and associated functions woman is not the decision maker in the household, particularly major decisions pertaining to agricultural land, house construction, children's marriage and the like.

To wind up the present empirical section, we hold that women as domestic labourers perform the double task of reproduction viz., social and biological, however this reproduction is not necessarily oppressive uniformly The structuring of social relations inhibit or slow or blur the collective consciousness and finally contribute to the oppression of women. In an oppressive and class ridden society objective consciousness of domestic labour does not necessarily transform into subjective consciousness, because domestic labour is not specific to the reproduction of one class but to the reproduction of opposing classes. Historically gender based subordination has curtailed women's access and control to resources and labour power and imposed sexual division of labour. However the subordination of women vary across region, classes and castes in time and space. Besides gender subordination is deeply internalized by both the sexes and more often viewed as a natural corollary of the biological differences between the sexes. It is transmitted and enforced through different cultural norms, beliefs and education system giving rise to various forms. With the result sexual division of labour is perceived as natural fostering domesticity.

4

Summing Up

The dominance of merchant capital, the impoverisation of the peasants, slow rate of proletarianisation and separation of direct producers from the means of production, demographic pressures, landreforms and other like constraints bear on the limited growth of capitalism in agriculture. On the other side green revolution engineered agricultural growth progressed along with proletarianisation. Here eviction of small tenants along with labour migration from stagnant agricultural areas have enhanced the proportion of agricultural labour. Then it may be observed that this rising phenomenon of proletarianisation is the result of separation of direct producers from the means of production . The data from the present study show that there is a rising phenomenon of depeasantisation as 70% of them possessed land before they became migrant workers in Surat. Further our data also show that landlord-money lender factor and survival needs force the people to industrial setup as wage labour. The question of women in the present study needs to be perceived from this backdrop as they have migrated to Surat through the most influential and informal but institutional power structure called marriage. As women are located in the family, they are easily available as a disposable labour power source in the crisis of capitalism and the corresponding labour needs. However the thesis of reserve army labour remains problematic and incomplete to explain the dynamics of capitalism. In fact for Marx every wage worker belonged to the category of reserve army of labour both male and female.Thus considering general patterns of labour in some sectors the reserve army thesis becomes a historical conjecture than assertion. The point is that if men are affected by the restructuring process under capitalism, women are equally too.

Under the prevailing political economy it is erroneous to presume that family household unit persists due to the interests of capitalism. Family cannot be analysed merely from economic and ideological requirements of capitalism. (Hemphries 1977; Caulfield 1974). Much work is required on the redefinition of family relationships and the changes in the definition of work and women's place from the point of material changes in the economy. Because family unit directly responds to the changes in the organization of production and varies in time and space. Besides the contribution of the family in capitalism eventually becomes a product of the contradiction implicit in its relationship with capital.

In this connection it may be mentioned that the regulation of female sexuality is a feature of almost every social formation, though in diverse ways depending on the patterns of kinship, economic and political relations. The family is created by the rule of private property and reflects on the relations of production. The family is the central site of the oppression and an organising principle of the relations of production. For specific combination of gender and class relations entrench gender division in the fabric of social relations (Pathy 1987). However gender identity does not necessarily occur in family alone, but also in the educational institutions, religion and mass media which reproduce, recreate, modify and endorse through ideology. Thus men and women are socially and ideologically constructed rather than naturally given but they exist historically as *concrete beings*.

Specific mode if production fosters violence and this can be understood with relation to the role of women in family. Family consumes goods, reproduces the workers, sustains them and enables to inculcate children and adults alike the values required to maintain the legitimacy of the prevailing arrangements, while consumerism and commercialism overtake rest of the contradictions. Capitalism also polarises women to fulfill male-set standards of womanhood. Be that as it may labour processes do not exit in vacuum, but are embedded in specific modes of production. The process of maintenance and replacement of labour power is conflated under the term reproduction of labour power. Therefore we hold that social relations cannot be understood independent of specific historical processes. Accordingly family is not a timeless universal unit of human society (Vogel, 1978). Capitalism encourages male supremacy in order to stabilise reproduction of labour power as well as to keep the amount necessary labour at acceptable levels. Sexism legitimizes this family structure by defining women's position and their unpaid housework enables husbands and children to work for appropriators. Ultimately class nature of sexism is reproduced in the illegitimate market structure (Leonard, 1982) and systematises the oppression of women politically, economically and socially. In this connection mass media palys a vital role in shaping global culture by propagating dominant culture and oppressing women in subtle ways. The distortion of women as sexual objects in advertisements reinforces sexist attitudes by dehumanizing. Besides mass media also promotes sexist stereotypes dainty and feminine by implying that women's position is only in the home (women with washing machines, sewing machines, cookers, etc.) while men are portrayed as successful professionals. Furthermore massmedia reinforces men's concepts about women's place and role by legitimizing masculine dominance.

Meanwhile it is essential to note here while class forms as the organisation basis of capitalism, gender constitutes the hierarchical principle of patriarchy. Here lies the connection of the material basis of patriarchy. It deserves a mention here that patriarchy and the corresponding subordination of women is located in the mode of production of early peasant societies and its emergence predates the origın of private property (Meillassoux, 1981). Thus the emergence of private property in land is not a necessary production for its use as an object of labour. Thus even in subsitence societies (like some tribal communities like Lanjia Saoras, Khonds, etc.) we notice like coexistence of both individual and communal rights on land. Therefore we submit that the subordination of women just cannot be analysed in the framework of private property problematique. It is essential to cognize the historical relationship between gender and class. This way patriarchy and the sexual division of labour cut through family and economy. Patriarchy neither originated with capitalism nor it disappears with the overthrow of capitalism. Divsion of labour based on sex very much exists in socialist societies like Cuba and China though in different degrees. Accordingly patriarchy is cross-cultural and transhistorical phenomenon prevailing in different societies in varying degrees through institutionalization of sexual hierarchy. Men and women are exploited under capitalism as wage labourers; but with regard to women the oppression is both with the relations of production and also from the sexual hierarchy within and outside family: Women's oppression arises from production as well as reproduction as patriarchy and sexual division of labour rips through family and economy. Specific forms of oppression are articulated with in contextual structure of social relation.

Needless to mention that human consciousness is formed by the interplay between people as subjects and objects in the world in which they live. Social progress occurs through human labour and process of production and reproduction, the central features of human society. Accordingly women's oppression in social relations of production and reproduction stands vis-à-vis class oppression. Here gender permeates socio-political and economic organizations and gender relations are integral constituents of social organizations of class. Patriarchal household is the historical product of prolonged and uneven process by which pre-existing forces of subsistence relations get incorporated and adopted to the succeeding relations of production. The patriarchal principle is articulated to the larger socio-political and economic organization of the society and it cannot be separated from it (Paul, 1985). The social relations of reproduction are concentrated in the family and meet the requirements of relations of production. Therefore, the dynamics of family and the personal relations of power between husband and wife need to be perceived as a product of how family relations are organized beyond economic relations. Forms of family, work and living are integral for constructing and reconstructing class relations, particularly as the dominant class responds to changes in the forms of property relations, and in the organization of production. And therefore gender, as a category has to be applied along with the class lines in order to analyse women's oppression. Isolated from each other it runs the risk of simple description and reductionism. Dimension of sexuality, class nature of household and the specificity of oppression have to be analysed historically. However, we affirm that gender relations should not be reduced to the function of capital.

Be that as it may relations of production comprise gender division, caste, class and types of labour. Here it is essential to demarcate between the relations of production where gender plays a vital role and the means and forces of production (Barett, 1980). In order to measure quality of life of an individual (men or women) it is important to cognize the work hours spent informally (unpaid labour) as well as formal work hours. Precisely, as one of the criteria of a person's well being is the sum total of the labour and time invested both in work and in everyday life and the free time that is left over (Blekher, 1979). For, gender perceptions are produced and reproduced historically in cultural practices. Sex inequality reinforces class inequality, while class decisions are accentuated by gender discrimination. Therefore, we submit that class and gender are central to the analysis of women's oppression. Gender identity is created spontaneously, recreated continually, endorsed and modified through a series of internalisation processes. Sexual division of labour in the family and unequal relations between men and women are the impounding structures in family life, and accordingly her oppression is complete on her *entirety* i.e., mind, body and labour. In this connection it may be noted that the content, degree and the value of domestic work varies from society to society, region, class, caste and community depending on the level of development of productive forces and its relations.

The evidence from the study indicates that the interests of men and women vary though belonging to the same household. And this becomes all the more clear when the women do not have access to paid work. Women do not have access to economic assets directly but through males. We infer that gender gets politicized in changing phases of capitalism and restructuring. The variation in sexual division of labour is produced by its rigidity whether the work is "prescribed" or "preferred". At the outset it appears that development intensified inequalities since recently. In brief the implications of development have sharpened social identities and created cultural politics. However, caution is required in glorifying the local mores precisely as the deconstruction of colonial mind-set is Sisyphean task, a struggle against the entrenched culture of imperialism and this has to be fought at two fronts-at the specific and general levels. The study also pointsout that subordination of women lies in its relationship to men and the latter's over women and children which is legitimised. Furthermore, we also observed that pre-capitalist and capitalist relations co-exist both at home and work as the women are "permitted" to work outside the household but with restrictions on time and space; they are free to buy household items (like utensils and other associated accessories), while they are restricted in buying bigger deals of other such expenditures and it is invariably the males who decide on these important issues. As elsewhere the property whether it is the agricultural land or house is exclusively on the name of males only. Thus during domestic outbursts more often than not the house often than not the women only are insulted time and again to "get out". By the way this type of sensitive clash cuts across caste, class, community, ideology, level of education and profession. Unfortunately this vital qualitative data cannot be gathered as domestic disputes confine to the four walls of the house.

The study also reveals that the increase in women's paid work is due to the increase of marginalization of the rural households engaged in subsistence production. Due to demographic pressures on income and consumption pattern of the rural households, the structure of subsistence production undergoes change. Subsequently the decrease in the level of consumption necessitates the family members to pool in income - thus arises the increase of women in paid work force. The vast chunk of female wage labour comes from the landless and small peasant classes and are unskilled labourers whose wages are unequal with relation to males. Inspite of their share in contribution of resources , women do not have control over their labour power.

By way of closing inconclusively it may be pointed that the nature and form of domestic labour vary according to the given mode of production of which the former is a component. There is a complex dialectical relationship between production and reproduction. It needs a special mention that the public and private domains are structured because domestic labour in some form or other is universal but reflects differently according to different modes of production.

In the ultimate analysis women have to struggle at two levels i.e., along with other disadvantaged sections of society for social transformation and separately as women's movement is necessary to redefine their identities which is a continuous process. In this context the vast database on women since 1980s can generate a valuable information and identify critical and sensitive policy issues as well as new frontiers of research concerns. History reveals us to finite closures of diagnosis and induce us to see the developing present mostly in terms of the determining past. The tenor and tone in the present imbroglio reiterates complete human liberation. Too much optimism...

References

Alavi, H. (1978), "Peasants and Revolution" in A. R. Desai (ed.). *Rural Sociology in India*, Bombay: Popular Prakashan.

Ardner, E. (1972), "Belief and the Problems of Women" in Jean, S.F. (ed.). *The Intepretation of Ritual : Essays in Honour of A.I.Richards.* London : Tavistock.

Aries, Philippe (1962), *Centuries of Childhood: A Social History of Family Life.* London.

Beechey, V. (1979), "On Patriarchy" *Feminist Review,* No. 3.

Beechey, V. and Allen, R. (1982), *The Women Question.* U221 Unit 1; Milton Keynes : Open University Press.

Becker, G. (1965), "A Theory of Allocation of Time" *The Economic Journal.* Vol. LXXX, No. 200; pp. 493-517

Beneria, L. (1979), "Reproduction, Production and the Sexual Division of Labour" *Cambridge Journal of Economics.*Vol.3, No. 3.

Bennet, T. (1982), *Formalism and Marxism,* New York, Methuen

Benston, M. (1969), 'The Political Economy of Women's Liberation", *Monthly Review,* reprinted in Ellen Malos *The Politics of House Work,* London: Allson and Bushy, 1980.

———(1975), *Marx's Early Writings,* London.

Blekhen, Flagia (1979), *The Soviet Woman in the Family and in Society.* New York : John Wiley and Sons

Blumenfeld E. and Susan, M. (1980), "Domestic Labour and the Reproduction of Labour Power : Towards an Analysis of Women, The Family and Class" in B. Fox (ed.). *Hidden in the Household.* Toronto : The Women's Press

Brugel, Irene (1978), "What Keeps the Family Going ?" *International Socialism,* Series 2, No.1.

Brycasas, D. and Mbilin, N. (1979), "The Changing Role of Tanzanian Women in Production" Jipemoye 2, Dar Es Salam.

Buvinic, M. and N.H. Yousseff (1978), "Women-Headed Households: The Ignored Factor in Development Planning" Report submitted to AID/ID, International Centre for Research on Women, Washington.

Campbell, B. (1980), "Feminist Sexual Politics" *Feminist Review*, Vol.5.

Caplan, P. and Bujra, J.M. (ed.) *Women United and Women Divided*. London: Tavistock.

Caplan, T. (1954), *The Sociology Work*.New York : McGrawHill

Caulfield, M.D. (1974), "Imperialism, The Family and Culture of Resistance" *Socialist Revolution*, No.20, 67-85.

Cheater, Aglea P. (1989), *Social Anthropology*, London: Unwin Hyman

Coward, E. (1980), *Irrigation and Agricultural Development in Asia*, London.

Creighton, Colin (1985), "The Family and Capitalism in Marxist Theory" in Martin Shaw (ed.) *Marxist Sociology Revisited*. London: Macmillan.

Crossby, F.J. (1982), *Relative Deprivation and Working Women*. New York : Oxford University Press.

Davis, D. (1973), "Anthropology and Colonialism" *Current Anthropology*, Vol. 14.

Dalla Costa, M. and James, S. (1972), *The Power of Women and the Subversion of the Community*. Bristol : England.

Das, B. (1994), *Socio-economic Study of Slums in Surat City*. Surat. Centre for Social Studies.

Deere, C.D. (1979), "Rural Women's Subsitence Production in the Capitalist Periphery" in Rubin and Cohen, et.al. (ed.) *Peasants and Proletarians*. New York : Monthly Review Press.

Dhanagare, D.N. (1974), "Social Origins of Peasant Insurrection in Telangana". *Contributions to Indian Sociology*, No. 8, pp. 109-134.

Douglas, M. (1970), *Risk and Blame: Essays in Cultural Theory*, New York : Oxford University Press.

Edholm, F. (1977), "Conceptualising Women" *Critique of Anthropology*, Nos. 9810; 101-30.

Elkan, Walter (1956), *The Employment of Women in Uganda* (mimeo).

Engels, F. (1972), *The Origin of Family Private Property and the State*. New York.

Fee, Terray (1976), "Domestic Labour : Analysis of Housework and Its relation to the Production Process", *Review of Radical Political Economy*, Vol.8;1-8.

Forster, R and O. Ranun (eds) (1976), *Family and Society* Baltimore: John Hopkins University Press.

Fruzzetti, L. (1982), *Concept of Person*, London.

Gardner, J. (1975), "Women's Domsetic Labour" *New Left Review*, No. 94; 85-96.

Goldthrope, J.H. (1983), "*Women and Class Analysis*. In defence of the Conventional View" *Sociology*, Vol. 17, No.14.

Goody, J. (1972), *Domestic Groups*. Addison-Wesley Module in Anthropology, 28.

———(1976), *Production and Reproduction, Cambridge* : Cambridge University Press.

Gough, K. (1955), "The Nayars and the Definition of Marriage", *Journal of Royal Anthropological Institute of Great Britain and Ireland*, 89 : 23-24.

Gramsci, A. (1971), *Selections from the Prison Notebooks*, London.

Griffiths, D. and Saraga, E. (1979), "Sex Differences in Cognitive Abilities : A Sterile Filed of Enquiry?" in O. Hartnett, *et.al. Sex-role Stereotyping*. London : Tavistock.

Harris, Olivia and Kate Young (1981), "Engendered Structures : Some Problems in The Analysis of Reproduction" in Joel Khan and L. Joseph (ed.). *The Anthropology of Pro-Capitalist Societies. London:* Macmillan.

Herskovits, M.J. (1955), *Cultural Anthropology*. London.

Humphries J. (1981), "Class Struggle and The Persistence of the Working Class Family" *Cambridge Journal of Economics* I (3): 241-58

Hymes, D. (1972), *Reinveting Anthropology*. New York: Random House.

Jennes, Linna (ed.). (1972), *Feminism and Socialism* Neew York: Panthoon Press.

Leach, E. (1958), "Bridewealth and Marriage Mobility", *Man*.

Leacock, E. (1979), "Women Development and Anthropological Facts and Fictions " in C.D. Deere (ed.). *Women in Latin America Revesside Latin American Press.*

Leeds, A. (1976), "Women in the Migratory Process: A Reductionist Outlook", *Anthropology Quaterly*, Vol.49, Jan.

Lenin, V.I. (1969), *What is to be done? Burning Questions of Our Movement*. New York : International Publishers.

Leonard, E.B. (1982), *Women , Crime and Society : A Critique of Theortical Criminology* , New York : Longman

Ma-feje, A. (1971), "The Ideology of Tribalism" *The Journal of Modern African Studies*, Vol.9.

Malinowski, B. (1927), *The Sexual Life of Savages*. London.

Marx, K. (1967), *Capital* Vol. I. New York : International Publishers.

———(1972), *Grundrisse*. New York

Mead, M. (1975), *Male and Female : A Study of Sexes in a Changing World*. Penguin Books.

Meillassoux, C. (1981), *Maiden, Meals and Money: Capitalism and the Domestic Economy*. Cambridge: University Press.

Mies, M. (1980), *Indian Women and Patriarchy : Conflicts and Dilemmas of Students and Working Women, New Delhi : Concept.*

Morokovasasic, M. (1981), "Sexuality and the Control of Procreation" in Young and Wolkowitz *(ed.) Of Marriage and the Market*. London: CSE Books.

Morton, A.L., (1952), English Utopia.

Oakley, A. (1974), *The Sociology of Housework*, New York : Pantheon Books.

Pathy, S. (1987), "Women,Violence and Structural Modalities", *The Eastern Anthropologist*. Vol.40, No.1

Paul (pathy), S. (1985), "The Economics of Women's Oppression" in Susheela Kaushik (ed.) Women's Oppression. New Delhi: Shakti Books.

Rao, M.S.A. (1986), "Sociology in the 1980s" in T.K.Oommen and P.N.Mukherjee(ed.) *Indian Sociology*. Bombay : Popular Prakashan.

Rao, G.R.S. (1975), *Regionalism in India: A Case Study of Telangana Issue*. New Delhi, S. Chand & Co.

Rapp, Rayna (1978), "Family and Class in Contemporary America : Notes Towards and Understanding and Ideology " *Science and Society*, 42,:3,278-300.

Reddy, V. (1977), "Cooli Dandu" Special Issue , Vijayawada.

Reiter, Rayna (ed.). (1975), *Towards and Anthropology of Women*. New York : Monthly Review Press.

Richards, T.F.(ed.) (1982), *Kinship and Authority in South Asia*, London: Allen and Unwin.

Roberts , P. (1981), "The Sexual Politicsd of Labour in Western Nigeria and Hausa Nigeria", C. Moser and K.Young (eds.). *Women and the Informal Sector*. IDS Bulletin, Vol. 12, No.3.

Rosaldo, M.Z. and Lamphere, L. (eds.). (1974), *Women, Culture and Society* Standford: University Press.

Rowbotham, S. (1973), *Women's Consciousness, Man's World* , London: Penguin Books.

Russell, K. and Urry, J. (1982), *Social Theory as Science*. Melboune : Rotledge and Kegan Pual.

Saadwi, N.(ed.) (1980), *The Hidden Face of Eve. London : Zed Books.*

Sanjek, R. (1982), "The Organisation of Households in Adabraka: Towards a wider comparative Perspective" *Comparative Studies in Society and History* , Vol. 24; No.1,Jan.

Sharma, B.A.V., (ed.) (1980), *Political Economy of India: A Study of Land Reforms Policy in Andhra Pradesh*. New Delhi : Light and Life Publication

Standt, K.A. "Women Farmers and Inequities in African Services" *Rural Africa*, No. 29; African Studies Centre, Michigan.

Sundarayya, P. (1972), *Telegana People's Struggle and Its Lessons*. Calcutta: CPM Publications.

Tiger , Lionel. (1970), *Men in Groups*. New York : Vintage Publications.

Turner , R. (1968), *The Body and Society*. London.

Vogel, L. (1979), "Questions on the Women's Question", *Monthly Review*, 31:2, 39-59.

Vyas, V.S. (1970), "Tenancy in Dynamic Setting", *Economic and Political Weekly*, Vol. XX,No.42

Yalman, N. (1979), *Under the Bo Tree*. Barkley :University of California Press.

Young K. (1978), "Modes of Production and the Sexual Division of Labour : A Case Study from Oaxca , Mexico" in Kuhn , A and Molpe , A (ed.) *Feminism and Materialism* London Rouledge and Kegan Paul.

Zaretsky, E. (1976), *Capitalism , the Family and Personal Life*. New York: HArpa

Index